PRETTY POLY

ALEX IRELAND

PRETTY POLY

THE HISTORY OF THE FOOTBALL SHIRT

pitch

First published by Pitch Publishing, 2023

Reprinted, 2023 (2nd print run)

Pitch Publishing
9 Donnington Park,
85 Birdham Road,
Chichester,
West Sussex,
PO20 7AJ
www.pitchpublishing.co.uk
info@pitchpublishing.co.uk

A CIP catalogue record is available for this book from the British Library.

ISBN 978 1 80150 461 4

Typesetting and origination by Pitch Publishing

Printed and bound in India by Thomson Press

Contents

Preface

I'M NOT sure exactly when I became a football shirt fan, as opposed to just a follower of the beautiful game. As I write this, wearing one of around 80 long-sleeved 1990s club shirts in my collection (the 1996/97 Juventus third shirt, in case you were asking), it has clearly become more than a casual interest. I started the day – as usual – by quickly scanning through hundreds of auction site listings, trying to hunt down those jerseys which have evaded me so far. I now sit typing the latest of around 55,000 words assembled over more than a year working on this book. As I look around the room, I see my bookcase shelf bending under the weight of dozens of football shirt books, and the walls bare but for a series of football shirt illustrations and a framed Matthias Sammer jersey. It is at this point that I begin to think that perhaps this has got a little out of hand. So how did I become one of millions of global fans obsessed with these iconic garments, and end up writing this book?

A lifelong resident of Trafford, my dad first took me to Old Trafford as a nine-year-old during the 1992/93 season as Manchester United claimed their first top-flight title in 26 years. While I have followed the club ever since, it was in the late 1990s that my broader passion for football was ignited. The Reds reached further into the Champions League, and Channel 4's *Football Italia* and Sky's La Liga coverage brought live foreign football into our home for the first time. To an impressionable teen, players such as Ronaldo, Gabriel Batistuta, Hristo Stoichkov and Roberto Baggio seemed impossibly glamorous compared to what felt like a relatively parochial Premier League.

Almost from the start I was drawn to a romantic image of the game, like when an Ajax team containing eight youth-team products beat AC Milan's star-studded side in the 1995 Champions League Final. Modern football economics makes this sort of feat almost impossible, but similar stories later in the decade would fascinate me. For example, Dynamo Kyiv's youth-team product and future Ballon d'Or winner Andriy Shevchenko scoring eight goals in ten post-qualifying games to fire the team to the 1998/99 Champions League semi-final, before leaving for AC Milan for $25m. Often teams who I had viewed at close hand as they dispatched my beloved United would attract my attention, such as the victorious Borussia Dortmund side led by Matthias Sammer in 1996/97 or Monaco's young team in 1997/98. Sammer in particular stood out, his barnstorming performances in the exotic *libero* role a world away from the rigid 4-4-2 I watched every week.

Being an enthusiastic amateur footballer, I was keen to take the field wearing the exotic strips sported by these teams. Unfortunately, in the early days of the internet, shirt fans were almost wholly dependent on the buyers at high-street store JJB

Sports to determine the strips available to them. As a result, I had to be a little more creative to acquire these objects of my footballing affection. I remember ordering a Monaco home strip via a telephone call to the club shop using schoolboy French in 1999 or so.

At the turn of the millennium, availability improved through the likes of Subside Sports, who advertised in the *World Soccer* magazines that had become my bible. Having been struck by a new team or player such as Gaizka Mendieta, who fired Valencia to consecutive Champions League finals in 2000 and 2001, I would add the relevant strip. In particular, the achievements of emerging 'wonderkids' such as Atlético Madrid's 18-year-old Fernando Torres, less than four months my junior, would catch my eye, leading to me purchasing the club's 2002/03 home kit. At the time, Real Madrid's collection of world-class stars such as Luís Figo, Zinedine Zidane and Ronaldo made them the most glamorous team on the planet and their Siemens-sponsored Adidas shirt was soon in my wardrobe.

There was no idea of collecting, preserving or doing anything else with the shirts other than sporting them on the five-a-side pitch before chucking them in a hot wash. Given this attitude, it is a miracle that while there were some casualties (a Kappa Sampdoria Antonio Cassano strip unfortunately among them), so many of the shirts survive intact to this day. Of note is a beautiful long-sleeved Juventus 2002/03 European home shirt, its 'DAVIDS 26' print and felt details remaining almost as new despite its thick fabric having made it a regular comfort on games in cold Manchester winter nights. This is a testament to the quality of shirts at that time, early Nike 1990s strips in particular being almost indestructible.

Like many football fans of my generation, I was also hopelessly addicted to the *Championship Manager* computer game which also fed my enthusiasm for little-known teams and players and led to my most embarrassing kit-related moment. In 2006, I spent 20 minutes on the phone trying to persuade a bemused Millwall club-shop employee to print a full kit with the name and number of youth player Cherno Samba. He was yet to make an appearance for the club, but in the imaginary world of the Collyer brothers' creation he had scored over 1,000 goals under my virtual watch, leading Millwall and England to multiple triumphs.

Having continued naively in this vein for years, it wasn't until my friend Matt Leach highlighted a few Twitter posts online in 2017 or so that I realised that other people had a passion for shirts. Further to that, links he'd send me to online retailers showed me an opportunity to fill in key gaps in my collection. Initially through my work-related Twitter account and then from a dedicated account I became a part of the online community of shirt fans. This accelerated in early 2020 as the Covid-related lockdowns led to an explosion in interest in football shirts.

Like many collectors, my collection has evolved and now – for the sake of my marriage and bank balance – I have focused on only these long-sleeved club shirts from the 1990s, that crucial period where my interest in football and kits exploded. With patience, daily eBay searches and some tip-offs from fellow collectors I have been fortunate enough to acquire some incredible shirts that I would never have dreamed of owning when I began. A 1997/98 Fiorentina Nintendo shirt as sported by Argentinian striker Gabriel Batistuta, Borussia Dortmund's beautiful white 1996/97 European away shirt (never worn in a competitive game), and home and away VfL Bochum 1997–1999 *regenbogen* (rainbow) shirts are among the highlights. In particular, I have a soft spot for Nike's 1990–2000 series of Borussia Dortmund shirts and own 13 of the 15 they released commercially in long sleeves. Only the 1990/91 home and 1994/95 away shirts continue to elude me, along with the unreleased 1990–1994 away shirts.

During my university days I had harboured dreams of being a football journalist and had organised some post-graduation work experience but changed course eventually into academia. I had also run a small website after graduation featuring a series of match reports, but largely my writing experience was focused on the dry, ultra-rigorous format of scientific journal articles. In 2021 I began to work writing and editing pieces on football kits for fanzines and websites, such as an article on the effect of kit colours on performance. I really enjoyed the process of researching the topic and weaving it together into an article, without the prospect of facing the harsh panel of professional critics that I would encounter in my work-related publications.

I have written around a dozen pieces on topics ranging from the Nike-era Borussia Dortmund strips, to interview-led pieces with retailer Classic Football Shirts (CFS) and the excellent Manchester-based kit manufacturer Hope and Glory. The highlight so far has undoubted been publishing an article on Finnish side HJK Helsinki in *World Soccer*. Seeing my piece in the magazine I used to read cover to cover in adolescence was a real bucket-list moment. The whole process of getting a physical press pass, watching from the media section, and interviewing CEO and ex-Crystal Palace player Aki Riihilahti was an incredible experience.

Having read websites such as Historical Football Kits and Museum of Jerseys, and books on kits such as John Devlin's renowned *True Colours* series and Stefan Appenowitz's excellent *Bundesliga Trikots* book, I thought there was a space for a book to tell the story of the history of the football kit. It would detail how the garment changed from an everyday shirt to the technological marvel of today, how sponsors and numbers came to be added and the remarkable story of the emergence and growth of the replica kit industry. With encouragement from pal Rob Fletcher who had also started writing articles on football kits, I submitted a proposal to Pitch Publishing in February 2022 and they agreed to publish the book. The past year has consisted of interviewing kit experts, trawling websites, books and archive material to pull together the story. It has been an amazing experience, and I have loved learning even more about the evolution of this beloved garment.

At this point I wish to issue a pre-emptive apology. While I have made substantial effort to document key moments in kit history which occurred outside the UK, there is only so much that a smattering of schoolboy French, Italian and German and Google Translate can accomplish in tandem. As discussed, my passion is in the battles between leading clubs and hence top-tier professional sides are covered more extensively than lower-league teams. As a result, there are many fascinating subplots of the tale which are not covered within the confines of this single volume. This includes goalkeeper shirts, which have their own story – one also well worth telling.

With those caveats in place, I sincerely thank you for taking the time to read this book, and hope that you enjoy reading it as much as I did putting it together. It has been no small amount of work, but it has at every stage felt like a privilege to be able to tell this fascinating story.

Introduction

TAKEN OUT of context, a football shirt is an unremarkable garment. Made of cheap polyester in low-pay conditions, its fast-fashion base is embellished with the brand mark of any one of several faceless sportswear firms. These are partnered with crests that have been increasingly stripped of their historical meaning to create seamless online 'brand identities'. But when put into the context of its on-pitch appearances, it is transformed into a precious, nostalgia-soaked relic. England's grey 1996 kit (officially listed as 'indigo blue') recalls a golden summer when Cool Britannia met football's march into the mainstream, while the geometric patterns of the Netherlands' 1988 kit bring to mind Marco van Basten's inch-perfect volley and the belated realisation of this small nation's extraordinary pool of talent.

Even the mention of the sponsor names instantly conjures up key sporting moments. Die Continentale means the recall of a neon-clad Matthias Sammer driving his Borussia Dortmund team-mates to Champions League glory, while Newcastle Brown Ale brings memories of Kevin Keegan's electrifying Newcastle United side failing to stop Sir Alex Ferguson's trophy-hogging juggernaut. As leading football historian Professor

Jean Williams described to me, 'Kit is really important and integral to the history of football. It's not a peripheral subject, it's absolutely central.'

The shirt has become a sacred relic of the game and a key part of footballing vocabulary, as Gavin Kendall and Nick Osbaldiston described in 2010. The harshest assessment levelled at underperforming players is that they are 'not fit to wear the shirt', an insult which surfaces in mid-match chants. Underpinning this idea, two of Hertha Berlin's players were forced to take off their jerseys and lay them in front of their supporters as a sign of their inadequacy after a 4-1 loss to city rivals Union in 2021. Those players who do not appear to be able to handle the pressure at a high-profile club are similarly described as 'struggling with the weight of the shirt'.

Such is the item's significance that being seen to disrespect the garment itself is one of the most heinous crimes a footballer can commit. When Arsenal's Swiss international captain Granit Xhaka threw his club jersey to the ground after being substituted in October 2019, the consequences were severe. He was stripped of the captaincy, and three years later he described his relationship with the Gunners' fans as still being fractured despite huge improvements in his and the club's form. The shirt is often a central piece of goal celebrations, players kissing the badge to show their devotion to the club or pointing to their own name and number as an act of self-promotion. It can also act as a token of mutual respect in the post-match exchange of shirts by players (described later in the chapter 'The Collector') who only minutes earlier were engaged in a physical and technical battle.

Beyond the football pitch, the cultural importance of shirts is demonstrated by their use to mark the most important life events. In 2018, Bergamo side Atalanta began sending a shirt to every newborn baby in the local area in an attempt to connect with the local community and attract new followers. Situated only 35km from Milan in a city of 120,000 habitants, the club have struggled to retain their local fanbase while living in the shadow of the two Milanese mega clubs. This strategy was also adopted in 2022 by Italian microstate San Marino, the lowest-ranked FIFA national side whose population of 35,000 is smaller than the ground capacities of many of the stadiums in which they play. Periodic newspaper articles show fanatical supporters wearing their team's strip on their wedding day, inevitably accompanied by a photo of their spouse smiling wanly as their own traditional dress stands in stark contrast to their partner's choice of lurid polyester. The garment's use even extends beyond life, with other fans choosing to go to their final resting place clad in this memento of their lifelong obsession.

Given the antipathy between fans, football shirts have also been weaponised to antagonise supporters of a rival club. Photos of Liverpool icon Steven Gerrard and Tottenham Hotspur's all-time top scorer Harry Kane wearing Everton and Arsenal strips respectively as children are regularly posted in an attempt to render their years of accomplished service somehow inauthentic. Shirts buried in the foundations of stadiums occupied by Liverpool, Portsmouth, Coventry and Manchester City by rival fans employed in their construction act as a permanent claim on enemy territory.

In addition to its sporting significance, the football shirt has become part of a huge global business. This is in large part thanks to the growth of the replica shirt industry, which Leicester firm Admiral established in the 1970s. Crucial, too, was the introduction of shirt sponsorship which also began to develop rapidly from the same decade. The Premier League 'big six' – Manchester United, Manchester City, Liverpool, Chelsea, Arsenal and Tottenham – receive an estimated £350m per season from their kit suppliers, plus £250m from front-of shirt sponsors and an additional £70m from sleeve sponsors. The £132m received by Manchester United alone (£75m Adidas kit deal, £47m TeamViewer front-of-shirt sponsor, £10m DXC sleeve sponsor) is greater than the £129m received by the other 14 Premier League clubs outside the big six combined. Individual replica shirts retail at over £110, despite production costs of around five per cent of that figure.

The popularity of vintage shirt collecting means that sought-after classics such as the 1988 Netherlands home and 1991/92 Barcelona away shirts cost nearly £1,000 on the rare occasion that they appear for online auction. This is nothing compared to the prices of famous match-worn shirts, Diego Maradona's jersey from the 'Hand of God' match against England in 1986 fetching £7.1m at auction in 2022.

Football shirts represent a key part of the sport's financial growth over the past half a century, and in turn the inequalities both between and within leagues which threaten the modern game. When considering the huge environmental impact of shirt production and the widespread mistreatment of factory workers, the industry could be seen as an example of the worst excesses of 21st-century capitalism. This is a far cry from the birth of the game when so low was the garment's financial, cultural and sporting value that not even its colour was considered important.

The Shirt

LIKE ANY other institution, football does not exist in a vacuum. It has always been strongly influenced by the economic, political and technological state of the wider world and this extends to developments in the humble football shirt. In this context, it is important to remember that organised football as we know it is a modern invention at a little over 150 years old. Association football was only formally codified for the first time in 1848 with the more widely accepted 'Sheffield rules' being written in 1858. The world's first football club, Sheffield FC, had been formed the previous year, and in England the Football Association (1863), FA Cup (1871), international football (1872), legalisation of professionalism (1885) and the Football League (1888) all emerged within just 30 years. As you will see throughout the book, key developments in shirt design resulted from these rapid changes in football itself or commonly in response to events in the wider world. These varied from the advent of legalised football professionalism to the invention of television and even the passing of the UK's Copyright Act in 1968.

As kit was not considered an important part of football in the early days of the sport, few direct contemporary references are available whereas in later years items like league handbooks provide robust evidence. Researchers are dependent on evidence such as match reports from newspapers, manufacturer and retailer catalogues, and black and white photography, the latter making aspects such as shirt colours hard to define. Dave Moor is a kit expert who founded and runs the Historical Football Kits website, maintained by an army of amateur researchers. The site tracks the history of football shirts, with a primary focus on British club and international sides. Dave described the early evolution of the football shirt. Initially, there were no team kits and players would use a cap or sash to mark out one team from another. Players would wear whatever garment they had to hand, with cricket whites commonly being worn as regular players sought a winter sport. As uniform kits began to emerge in the 1870s, they were initially the preserve of teams of players from wealthier backgrounds due to the cost of paying a tailor to construct a custom garment. The shirts would be made by independent manufacturers, meaning there was substantial variation evident even within teams.

The National Football Museum regularly displays a jersey worn by Arnold Kirke Smith of Oxford University in football's first international match, England v Scotland in 1872. Casting aside its place as one of the most precious relics of the game, what strikes the viewer is how ordinary the garment is. Save for the embroidered three lions crest, the woollen shirt with its low-profile collar and thick cuffs looks like winter underwear rather than an artefact at the heart of the game's birth. In several early England internationals, including the team's first meeting with

Wales in 1879, the players wore their own club jerseys. Press criticism of the players' mismatched outfits in that game was the catalyst for the FA's decision to finally supply players with standard shirts later that year.

The codified game of association football grew initially from public schools. University and workplace teams founded and populated by graduates from these institutions dominated the early club competitions. However, the game quickly spread to the wider population, evidenced by Blackburn Olympic's FA Cup win in 1883. This working-class side, composed largely of northern factory workers, was very different to the wealthy Home Counties amateur teams that had captured the first 11 FA Cups. In particular, the club provided jobs for players and offered additional payments to supplement their income. While the newer northern clubs swiftly pushed for legalisation of professionalism, the FA initially resisted the move away from the amateur ideal.

This would become a recurring theme as football associations across the globe continued to show a conservative attitude to changes in the game. It was only when a group of around 30 clubs including Aston Villa, Preston North End and Newton Heath (later to become Manchester United) formed a breakaway British Football Association that the FA relented. The advent of legalised professionalism in 1885 led to unified team kits as clubs began to provide equipment for their players. Being mindful of their costs, they would often pick simple, cheaper designs. 'I find the social history of this topic fascinating,' said Dave Moor. 'To see how the game developed from its roots in the public schools and became taken up by the working classes and the impact that had on aspects like the design of football kits was significant.'

The emerging market for team sportswear was served by new firms such as Bukta in 1879, meaning that mass-produced outfits were available for the first time. Shirts were commonly sold by the dozen, and available in a variety of fabrics. Flannel or worsted wool knit was a common option available in different grades, with more expensive cashmere shirts also available although these could cost 50 per cent more than the basic versions.

At this point, it is appropriate to highlight the pioneering role that British football played in development of the game. The move to overt professionalism was decades ahead of other leading modern football nations such as Italy and Spain (1926), France (1932), Argentina (1931), Brazil (1933) and West Germany (1963). In many cases, development of the game in these countries was led by British immigrants across the social strata. The British FAs retained this sense of superiority even when other nations had developed beyond them. This may explain why the association and teams were slow to adopt later innovations in areas such as shirt sponsorship.

While trends in shirt colours changed over the following decades as described in 'The Colour' later in this book, there was little innovation in the basic design over that period. The shirt was a purely functional garment used to clothe the player, and from 1891 to identify their team as club colours were mandated by the Football League. The concept of performance design was still a long way off, as players trudged round in heavy, ankle-high leather boots whose primary purpose was protection.

This is not to denigrate the physical ability of the early players presented unsmiling in unfamiliar outfits in Victorian team photos. Footage from the Mitchell and Kenyon collection recorded at the turn of the 20th century shows a dynamism that is surprising given that their outfits appear better suited to the factory floor than the football pitch. While the videos betray some tactical and technical naivety, clips of mazy dribbles, rifled shots, and crunching tackles show no lack of physical talent. The frantic appeals to the referee seemingly over each decision would also be very familiar to the modern fan. There was little commercial impetus to adapt shirts in the absence of a replica shirt industry, and the concept of a 'brand identity' was not developed. Therefore, in the absence of a strong motive for innovation, changes were largely confined to minor design tweaks. For example, around the turn of the 20th century laced collars became popular in England, only being replaced by the familiar rugby-style collar in the 1930s.

In addition to the development of the men's game, women's football was also growing in the UK with the first international match played between Scotland and England in May 1881. A replay of the match later that month attracted over 5,000 fans, and the inaugural fixture of one of the first women's club sides, British Ladies' Football Club, took place in front of a crowd of over 10,000 spectators in 1895. As in many areas, the development of shirts for female football players has received a lot less attention than those of the men.

Professor Jean Williams, an expert in the history of football and the women's game, detailed the development of shirts for female players from the Victorian period onwards. The Rational Dress movement of the middle and late Victorian era promoted simpler, more comfortable and functional clothing like split skirts, bloomers or pyjama trousers as part of a move towards sex equality. Although these developments were not widely adopted in everyday clothing until after the First World War, they did take hold in women's football. Looking at pictures of British Ladies' Football Club founded by the pioneering Nettie Honeyball, the players wear football boots, shin pads, bloomers and baggy shirts. 'That was a little bit different to what was happening with rational dress in different contexts,' explained Professor Williams. 'For example, women who would wear it to cycle in the street were sometimes attacked for being seen in public.' In contrast, this very male silhouette became established as women's footballing 'uniform'.

The popularity of women's football in England increased dramatically during the First World War, as women replaced the men who had gone to the frontline. This was in the workplace as they were recruited as police and fire officers, transport conductors and particularly munitions factory workers, but also to replace the entertainment of men's football. This would mean that in many workplaces, much simpler, more 'male' items such as trousers and suits were worn for performance and safety. This led into football as women's teams began to wear coloured jerseys in similar styles to those of the men, complemented now by shorts and stockings making the two sexes almost indistinguishable. Threatened by the popularity of the women's game, the Football League pressured the Football Association to ban it. This was put in place in 1921, when women were prevented from playing football at any Football Association-affiliated club or facilities until 1969.

The FA considered football unsuitable for women, despite their demonstrated ability to complete a full week's factory work in place of men before playing at the weekend. Many of the wartime matches played by women had raised large sums of money for charities including for injured servicemen. After the war, the type of causes expanded to include support for the families of striking miners. It has been suggested by some historians that this move to support working-class people may have contributed to government pressure to implement a ban. Despite the ban, some large organisations including retailer Marks & Spencer organised women's work teams from the 1930s – these teams would play in simple men's kits. Thereafter, women participating in amateur leagues and competitions would adopt the fit and design of the men's team shirts due to a lack of alternatives.

At the start of the 1950s, football shirts were largely indistinguishable from those worn at the turn of the century. However, a series of technological, political and social changes inside and outside the game would lead to substantial changes in the following decade. The first innovation was floodlighting and evening matches. While floodlit matches date back to 1878, they were limited by the reliability of batteries and generators. Arsenal manager Herbert Chapman had permanent lights installed at Highbury in the 1930s, but the FA initially refused to sanction their use during Football League and FA Cup matches. The advent of the National Grid in 1938 improved convenience and reliability, and Southampton became the first club to install floodlights, in 1950, although the primitive systems were only partially effective.

To improve visibility, Manchester United and Wolverhampton Wanderers pioneered the use of reflective kits made from artificial materials like rayon. Kits had previously been made from natural fabrics such as wool and latterly cotton, Umbro's Peruvian pima cotton 'Tangeru' fabric being an early example of technology branding when introduced in the 1930s. The new fabrics came to the fore in the 1953 'Stanley Matthews' FA Cup Final played under natural light, as Bolton Wanderers dazzled in a brilliant white Umbro rayon jersey. As the number of floodlit friendly matches increased, the FA eventually relented and the first nighttime England match (November 1955) and Football League game (February 1956) took place soon after. Unfortunately, the rayon shirts were less of a success with players, and the uncomfortable, sweat-retaining garments were phased out by the end of the decade.

The early growth of the game in the UK meant that matches were played in the cold British winter, reflected in the heavy, long-sleeved, collared shirts worn with a third of the garment being tucked into the shorts. The foundation of national leagues in Spain, Italy and France as well as the advent of international tournaments such as the Copa América (1916) and World Cup (1930) saw the development of the professional game in warmer climates and different cultures across the globe. As such, innovation increased as did the means by which new technologies and trends could be adopted by other teams.

Brazil, Cuba, the Dutch East Indies (now Indonesia) and Germany were the first World Cup sides to wear short-sleeved shirts, in 1938. Having finally adopted short sleeves in 1949, England were humbled in a 6-3 loss to Hungary in 1953 – their first defeat at Wembley. Like their tactics and technical ability, the visitors' lightweight shirt and deep V-neck (a style also worn by the likes of Uruguay and Real Madrid) seemed light years ahead of that of their opponents. Inspired by this, Umbro released a new 'Continental' style in 1954 which may be considered their first performance-focused design. Worn initially by England, it was then enthusiastically adopted by teams in the Football League and abroad.

Another innovation which has since dominated the development of football shirts is television. While live matches were broadcast in several countries in the 1930s, the limitations of transmission technology and the relatively low ownership of television sets meant that initial interest was low. However, both improved from the 1950s and live broadcasts of the 1954 and 1958 World Cups and the new European Cup from 1955 allowed fans to see foreign sides in action for the first time. While the commercial value of this exposure was yet to be realised, dominant sides such as Real Madrid and Brazil began to grow a global fanbase. Real's long-sleeved, crew-necked jersey was subtly marketed by Umbro as the 'Real' style and adopted by leading teams such as Manchester United and

Liverpool. Indeed, work led by Chris Stride from the University of Sheffield showed that 95 per cent of Football League teams wore collarless shirts by the mid-1960s up from only 20 per cent in the previous decade. The Real shirt was later more brazenly rebranded as 'Aztec' in the run-up to the 1970 World Cup in Mexico. The match between West Ham and Liverpool in 1969 was the first to be broadcast in colour, adding a new dimension to the technology, and influencing the bright colours and white shirts which would feature in the early 1970s.

The increased media exposure of football and rise of celebrity players also saw the shirt's silhouette begin to reflect prevailing fashion trends. Economic growth and the advent of rock 'n' roll and the teenager in the 1950s saw a revolution in high-street fashion, as a wider variety of less conservative clothing began to appear in the 1960s. Footballers also began to realise the commercial benefits of their increased exposure, aided in England by the abolition of the maximum weekly wage of £20 in 1961. Fulham star Johnny Haynes immediately became the first player to earn £100 per week, with Manchester United's George Best earning ten times that by 1968. The collarless fitted Real jersey matched with the sleek, simple 'mod' style of the 1960s, before broad collars made a return to the pitch and the high street in the 1970s with over 80 per cent of Football League teams sporting a collared shirt. This trend has continued to oscillate almost every decade since, and the fit of shirts has also waxed and waned in line with fashion. The skin-tight strips of the 1980s were replaced by ultra-baggy jerseys in the 1990s, as trends such as grunge and skateboarding culture were reflected in the acres of polyester which hung off even the largest players.

The now ubiquitous polyester was one of several innovations in clothing technology which began to impact on shirt designs in the final two decades of the millennium. As described later in this book, the birth of the replica shirt industry saw bolder, club-specific designs emerge for the first time in the 1970s. This was supported by the adoption of polyester shirts in the 1980s, which replaced cotton. Some teams had earlier worn lighter nylon shirts during the warmer months in place of traditional wool or cotton shirts. New sublimated printing techniques dramatically increased the range and complexity of designs which could be incorporated into shirts. Sublimation uses solid inks which turn into gas under heat, combining with the fabric to become permanently printed into the garment. The invention of the electronic Jacquard machine in 1983 soon permitted rich patterns to be woven into the fabric of the football shirt itself, with these jacquards adding another dimension to designs.

To combat the unfamiliar heat encountered in Mexico at the 1970 World Cup, England instead looked back to a technology invented in 1888. Manchester firm Aertex's perforated fabric had been used in British Army uniforms in hot climates, and in school wear including sportswear. Aertex worked on the principle that air trapped within the material would act as a barrier against warm and cold weather. Umbro licensed the technology and incorporated it into their Airtex shirts which were worn by Sir Alf Ramsey's team. The shirts were also adopted by the Scottish national side over the following decade, and by clubs including Liverpool, Arsenal and Rangers. Typically, the garments were worn in summer matches including competition finals and pre-season games.

Into the late 1990s, improvements in physical preparation saw the emergence of sports science and nutrition in football and the shirt was targeted in the pursuit of marginal gains. Gone were the heavy, patterned fabrics of the early part of the decade and in came the likes of Nike's Dri-Fit. Lighter than previous shirts, the material aimed to wick sweat away from the body rather than absorbing it and therefore weighing the player down. Unlike cotton, which can absorb nearly a tenth of its weight in water, polyester only absorbs less than one per cent.

However, displaying the remarkable ability of the football fan to be offended by change, this innovation came under fire from Boca Juniors fan and ex-governor of Buenos Aires, senator Antonio Cafiero. In a 1998 column in Argentina's largest newspaper, *Clarín*, he asked, 'How can we demand or implore our players to give everything on the field and soak their jersey with sweat if the jersey itself precisely prevents them from doing so? … I want a shirt that leaves a puddle on the locker room floor. That shows, with no shame, the result of honest work and being worn out.' The Dri-Fit shirt fabric also included SPF 30 protection against the sun's UV rays as another adaptation to warmer climates.

Player shirts began to feature ventilation holes and mesh panels to increase air flow and keep players cool. Into the new millennium, several brands (notably Kappa) introduced a skin-tight shirt aimed at reducing garment weight, although that ended up being a less flattering fit for the average fan. Indeed, at the birth of the sports science age of nutrition and fitness, norms were changing and for many players yet to adopt the new professional lifestyle these garments offered no hiding place. The shirts were made of materials like elastane, which is less breathable than polyester. However, they could stretch to several times their length before tearing, providing a closer fit and protection against shirt pulls.

American firm Nike have a long-held reputation for athlete-focused design, and they introduced several further innovations aimed at improving performance in the early 2000s. Craig Buglass and Ffion Appleton-Jones, two members of Nike's design team during this period, described some of the technologies they implemented. To help players cope with the heat in the 2002 World Cup in South Korea and Japan, the company launched dual-layer Cool Motion shirts. These were worn by the Nike-sponsored teams in the competition, although many of the United States players cut out the inner layer. 'We tried as hard as we could to convince them to take the kit [as it was] but they just wouldn't,' Buglass told ESPN in 2022. 'We were disappointed ... But if you look at any of the images [from the tournament] ... they are absolutely drenched.'

While they were successful in achieving their original aim, the shirts proved difficult for players to put on and take off, particularly when wet. This led to a couple of high-profile incidents, such as when Manchester United player Diego Forlán took off his shirt after scoring against fellow Premier League side Southampton in November 2002. Having been unable to put it back on, the Uruguayan played on topless for another 30 seconds, even managing a successful tackle on a Southampton player. At this point the referee halted the game and – with the aid of United's backroom staff – Forlán was helped back into his jersey. Nike also worked on the principle of 'zero distraction', aiming to ensure that the strip was as comfortable as possible so that players could concentrate solely on their football. To that end, the design team introduced bonded joints between the fabric segments in place of itchy sewn seams. While revolutionary and expensive at the time, bonded seams are now commonly used in player specification shirts.

As competition in the replica kit industry continued to grow, kit launches began to resemble more closely James Bond's gadget briefings by Q. Press releases gushed with details of space-age technologies able to unleash the wearer's innate and long-hidden potential. The fabric of Portsmouth's 2007/08 Canterbury 'IonX' shirt, in which they won the FA Cup and secured their highest league finish for over 50 years, contained a negatively charged electromagnetic field claimed to increase blood flow and oxygen levels. Harnessing advances in biomechanics, Adidas's 2010 World Cup Techfit kits were equipped with Powerweb technology, plastic bands which store and release elastic energy during movement. Throughout the decade the use of 'wearables' such as the Apple Watch, which tracked health-related data such as physical activity, heart rate and sleeping patterns, exploded into an industry worth over $100bn annually. This rise was reflected in Tottenham's 2011 deal with Under Armour, allowing them to include the firm's E39 biometric technology capable of recording body temperature, heart and breathing rate and of tracking players' movements.

Material features began to assume an active role, with Puma claiming that the ACTV tape introduced for Italy's 2014 World Cup shirts massaged muscles, increasing blood flow and endurance as well as stability. Even Hollywood became an inspiration, as Nike used the 3D motion capture underpinning CGI creations such as *The Lord of the Rings*' Gollum alongside body scans to identify the areas where sweat-wicking and more breathable regions were placed in player-issue shirts. More recently, Adidas's 2014 Climachill fabric contained spheres designed to cool players, made from aluminium and titanium, the same material from which the Terminator is hewn. Finally, an obsession with lightweight fabrics led to Puma's 2021 Italy ULTRAWEAVE shirt, at 72g the lightest football shirt ever and only around 40 per cent of the weight of the team's Euro 2020-winning shirt.

The arms race for technical superiority has led to changes in the fundamental laws of the game, as authorities look to keep pace with innovation. In 2002, the International Football Association Board (IFAB)'s Laws of the Game simply stated that players must wear 'a jersey or shirt'. For the 2002 Africa Cup of Nations, Puma designed a sleeveless shirt for Cameroon to reduce weight and prevent shirt-pulling. FIFA banned the kit in advance of that year's World Cup, communications director Keith Cooper stating, 'They're not shirts, they're vests.' The design also left nowhere for the tournament patches introduced for the competition to be applied. While Puma appealed and sought alternative solutions including temporary tattoos of the tournament logos, they eventually attached loose black sleeves to comply. The revised 2003 IFAB rules pointedly included the decision that 'jerseys must have sleeves', while the laws were finally adapted in 2008 to state that players required 'a jersey or shirt with sleeves'.

Puma and Cameroon continued to exploit ambiguity in the rules, with the team wearing a UniQT one-piece design for the 2004 Africa Cup of Nations. The result was criticism from the FIFA president, a £154,000 fine and a six-point World Cup qualifying-stage penalty. These were all later retracted after Puma issued a lawsuit, but the saga resulted in FIFA tightening their kit rules and insisting that countries submit their designs 12 months in advance of a tournament.

While the men's game saw massive commercial growth and innovation in kits throughout the second half of the 20th century, this was much less evident in the women's game. Having been forced to play in public spaces and being unable to charge spectators for nearly 50 years, the ban on women's football in England was gradually rescinded, beginning in 1969, with the ban on use of FA-affiliated facilities ending in 1971. Initially the Women's FA was set up like a county association and did not receive any funding, its first paid employee joining in 1981. The FA did not take over the running of the women's national team until 1993, and initially struggled to attract suppliers, relying on designs from smaller brands such as Spall and Ribero. Gillian Coultard, the first England women's player to 100 caps, wore an England men's shirt which was not cut for women and was much too big. The first women's World Cup did not take place until 1991, and in 1995 the USA team were the first team to wear a design distinct from the men's team.

The 2019 World Cup saw a revolution as most of the teams wore bespoke kits with separate designs to the men's team. Not only did the shirts feature different patterning, but they also incorporated female-specific design features requested by the players. This included a longer short sleeve to avoid exposing the whole upper arm, a wider neck to allow shirts to be put on over a ponytail and an altered fit to account for male–female differences in body shape. The US team's shirt went on to become Nike.com's best-selling single-season shirt of all time over the following year.

In 2004, the ever-progressive Sepp Blatter had offered his 'advice' to the nascent women's game, 'Let the women play in more feminine clothes like they do in volleyball. They could, for example, have tighter shorts … Female players are pretty, if you excuse me for saying so, and they already have some different rules to men, such as playing with a lighter ball. That decision was taken to create a more female aesthetic, so why not do it in fashion?' While these comments were rightly condemned, there have been concerns that commercial considerations are shaping the development of women's kit design in a way that does not best represent the playing community.

Professor Jean Williams noted that many female footballers have adopted a hyper-feminine silhouette adopted by the likes of Mia Hamm featuring 'the ubiquitous ponytail', perhaps in part to maintain sponsor interest. Nike and Adidas have adopted this narrow palette of femininity, using pinks, purples, flowers, and other very traditional stereotyped symbols of femininity in their designs. While this on its own is a legitimate component of femininity, its pervasiveness in current designs leaves little room for other types of female identity.

Professor Williams laments the lack of football-related iconography in women's design, in the same way that historical references appear to dominate the mood boards inspiring designers in the men's game, 'I like my shirt history, and I was a bit disappointed with some of the feminisation of design. There's long been a move to make things pink or purple if women are involved. Certain colours are very laden with symbolism and I didn't like the Euro 2022 shirts with floral patterns. They reminded me more of surfing motifs – why do we need to have flowery shirts because women are involved? I found some of the designs to be a bit predictable and not really originating from football history which is all about insignia, regalia, militarism, etc. Flowery football shirts are not for me!'

One potential contributing issue is the relatively short lifespan to date of the professional women's game. While many men's teams have over a century of uninterrupted history to call on, restrictions on women's football mean that the reservoir is much shallower. This is exacerbated by the fact that until recently women's teams shared kit designs with men and so the number of distinct kit references to draw upon is quite limited.

For so long, the long-sleeved jersey had been a characteristic feature of football, particularly in colder countries. However, Kevin Plank's Under Armour firm introduced close-fitting base layer garments which exploded in popularity in American sports around the millennium. As with football shirt technologies, the manufacturer claims are impressive, with oxygen supply to the muscle increased and the added support allowing players to turn more quickly. Manufacturers, particularly Nike with their Pro range, started to promote the garments in football – Manchester United's Wayne Rooney being a prominent early adopter around the time of the club's 2008 Champions League triumph. As a result, many players opted for short sleeves with these new garments underneath. This time IFAB were quick to act, and the 2008 laws stated, 'If undergarments are worn, the colour of the sleeve must be the same main colour as the sleeve of the jersey or shirt.' The new garments were an irritant for kit designers, as they often impaired the effectiveness of innovations such as venting or dual-layer designs.

The issue of sleeve length caused controversy at Arsenal in 2013, where there had been a long-standing tradition of the captain and kit man choosing the team's sleeve length. Midfielder Mathieu Flamini, a confirmed fan of short sleeves, crudely chopped the sleeves off his long-sleeved shirt for matches against Marseille and Manchester United. This caused him to receive a public dressing-down from manager Arsène Wenger and ex-player Lee Dixon, and behind closed doors he was apparently involved in a heated row with the Arsenal kit man Vic Akers. In February 2017, Theo Walcott defied the same tradition by wearing a short-sleeved shirt against the captain's choice for a Premier League match against Hull City. Again there was uproar from fans and ex-players but this proved to be the end for the long-held rule. Indeed, less than two weeks later Walcott retained his short-sleeved shirt when named captain for an FA Cup tie against Sutton United, although his team-mates all wore long sleeves.

The trend for short sleeves with or without base layers has become entrenched, such that by 2020 long-sleeved diehards such as Cristiano Ronaldo, Sergio Ramos, Gerard Piqué and James Rodríguez were firmly in the minority. Commercial pressures mean that many clubs now no longer offer long-sleeved shirts to players or fans. In the 2021/22 Premier League season, only Arsenal, Everton, Manchester City, Norwich City and West Ham made long-sleeved home, away and third shirts all available commercially in adult sizes. Manchester United offered a long-sleeve home shirt only, whereas for 14 clubs no long-sleeved shirt was available. Their demise is even more pronounced in continental Europe, where no Serie A side offered long-sleeved shirts in 2021/22 and Bayern Munich and Real Madrid were the only top clubs to offer fans an option on sleeve length.

Shorter sleeves are just one of the features that would render modern shirts unrecognisable to the Edwardian footballing pioneers. As we have seen throughout this chapter, economic, social and technological developments in the wider world have all at various points acted as agents of its evolution. As a result, the slim-cut, space-age materials and laser-cut features are now a world away from the baggy, functional and mismatching garments which clothed early players. But while the modern shirt now has its silhouette, and finally one that is distinct for men and women, it is, at this point in the story, a garment devoid of character and meaning. No player ever kissed a mesh panel in celebration. No fan's abiding first memory of the game is sweat-wicking fabric. The shirt itself has little to link it to a team, or a player, or a moment. The primeval emotions of joy, rage, despair and the unfailing devotion which football inspires need an equally ancient force to stimulate them. Something into which every fan can channel their hope, their loyalty, and their loathing. They need colour.

The Colour

A TEAM'S colours are a key part of their identity, and in several cases are distinctive enough to distinguish the side by themselves. Brazil's yellow shirt with green trim and blue shorts is unmistakeable, as are the likes of Monaco's red and white diagonal halves and Boca Juniors' blue shirt and yellow band. Even when rivals such as Manchester United and Liverpool share their colours, it does not diminish their fans' enthusiasm for their home strip. With this in mind, it is perhaps surprising that many teams adopted their current colourway 50 years or more after their foundation. Further than this, the concept of dedicated team colours was absent in the first decades of the game's development.

Sheffield FC, the world's oldest football club, were the first to designate kit colours in their 1857 rules, requesting, 'Each player must provide himself with a red and dark blue flannel cap, one colour to be worn by each side.' The first body to mandate team colours were the FA Cup Board, who in 1871 demanded the players of participating clubs appear in matching colours. The swift rise of working-class clubs after the FA's birth, particularly in the north, led to a sartorial clash on the pitch as well as economic disparity off it. While the 'gentlemen' club players could afford richly coloured, tailored shirts, teams from working backgrounds often wore mismatched kits in simple tones.

While many clubs adopted distinctive colours, the lack of a change strip or need to consider clashing designs caused substantial inconvenience to players and spectators alike. As one newspaper correspondent wrote following a Birmingham Association FA Cup game in 1879, 'In football it is a most essential point that the members of one team should be clearly distinguished from those of the other. The only way this can be effected is for each club to have a distinct uniform as the diversity of dress displayed yesterday not only confused the members of the team but the spectators were quite unable to say whether a man belonged to one team or the other.' This became more pressing as the game evolved from a focus on dribbling to passing, and the inclusion of offside in the first formalised rules in 1883 meant that identifying players was clearly key for officials.

The legalisation of professionalism by the FA and formation of the Football League in 1888 led to a move to simple kits in bright colours. This would serve to aid supporters, a new and increasingly important source of revenue, in identifying their team in packed grounds. Also, as the financial burden for kits now fell on clubs rather than players, for cost-conscious treasurers the simpler, cheaper designs were a natural choice. Kit manufacturers still provided for those with greater resources, as shown in a series of Victorian catalogues in the National Football

Museum archives. Sports equipment retailer W.G. Grenville of Birmingham sold a 'Merchant' design with three broad stripes in the body and three hoops down the sleeves. In contrast to the sombre impression given by black and white photographic records, these shirts were sold in bold combinations like the Bolivian (yellow, red and green) and a five-striped equivalent in royal blue, pink and green.

Kit clashes were not considered, which was highlighted in a match between Sunderland and Wolverhampton Wanderers in 1890, when both teams wore the same red and white stripes. This led the Football League, in 1891, to require clubs to declare their unique colours. Looking back, it seems remarkable that it took so long for this need to be addressed, coming 20 years after the foundation of the FA Cup. Following the ruling, Sunderland retained their kit colours, whereas Wolves adopted a now-familiar old gold with black, initially in a diagonal halved design. With the number of possible unique colours diminishing, the FA permitted teams to share colours. When colours clashed, the more newly founded team used a change strip in solid colour, which was usually white. The Football League later required that away sides wear their change strip from 1921.

The footballing world could have been a much less colourful place, if proposals at the Football League AGM by the Liverpool secretary for all home teams to wear red shirts (conveniently already Liverpool's colour) and away teams to wear white had been passed. However, in both 1904 and 1906 the motion was dismissed by Football League members. At the end of the First World War, a reduced supply of football kits meant that several teams adopted white kits, including Blackpool, who abandoned their red strip until 1923, thereafter taking up their distinctive tangerine for the first time. Similarly, rationing post-Second World War restricted teams' ability to purchase new kits and many adopted whatever styles were available – often relying on contributed coupons from fans.

In the 1950s, many clubs introduced an alternative (later known as a third) strip. While now seen as a money-making device by fans, this was originally introduced in case both home and change kits clashed. This sometimes arose in the FA Cup, where both teams were required to change in the event of a clash and would often have the same colour change kit. Into the 1970s, change strips were rebranded as away shirts and worn even in the absence of a clash in order to increase sales of the new fully branded replica kits.

Younger fans have grown up with the idea that kit colours are flexible, and that a team may turn up for home games in an away, third or even one-off shirt. This is reluctantly accepted as one of the many concessions to commercialism in the modern game. For fans like kit expert John Devlin, who has been watching matches since the 1970s, this represents an uncomfortable change from the days when these shirts would only appear in the event of a clash. 'Nowadays I feel quite alarmed by that as I see clubs' identities being eroded,' he explained the day after Tottenham Hotspur had worn a purple away kit rather than their white home kit in a match against a Manchester United side wearing their traditional red. 'If teams stuck with their colours it would make that identity so, so strong – it's so important! People say, "I don't care what they play in as long as they win." Really? In that case why not just have one team in red and one team in blue?'

Considering John's comments, this could represent part of the 'death by a thousand cuts' that the commercialisation of the game imposes. It seems a minor issue when comparing to the modern ills of ticket pricing, inconsiderate match scheduling, the erosion of local ownership, the fragmentation of TV deals and above all the threat to the existence of football competitions themselves posed by the likes of the scandalous European Super League initiative. However, making concessions to a club's fundamental on-pitch identity based on a potential hit to merchandise sales does seem like the thin end of the wedge in terms of core club concepts being at the mercy of commercial forces.

The relatively small number of teams competing in early international competitions limited kit clashes. However, even in the first World Cup in 1930, Bolivia were forced to change their white kit for a sky blue strip for their match against a Brazil side yet to adopt their iconic modern-day colourway. This was a shame, as the original strips each had a letter sewn on the front which spelled 'VIVA URUGUAY' in team photos as a tribute to their hosts. From 1950 to 1970, FIFA requested that national federations sketch the colours of their kit as part of the registration document. In 2014, the regulations were changed to mandate a dark and light kit and countries are now required to submit their designs 12 months in advance of a tournament. This process has since led to redesigns of several high-profile teams' kits, forcing Adidas to create a white kit for Spain's 2014

World Cup team after their home and away shirts were deemed too similar in colour. UEFA also insisted that Nike produce a revised white away kit for France's Euro 2016 team as the separate red and blue sleeves contravened their requirement that they be identical in colour.

Black shirts were finally permitted in the Premier League in 1992, as referees were given a teal kit with a black change shirt in case of a clash. This system was not foolproof, referee Alan Wilkie having to wear a white T-shirt the following season as Aston Villa's green and black striped away kit clashed with both strips. Colour regulations continue to be developed, Italy's Serie A outlawing green away/third kits due to the clash with 'green screen' virtual ad boards from 2022/23, although green home kits like Sassuolo's are exempt.

Despite regulations on kit colours being in place for well over a century, occasional kit clashes still occur, usually through human error. In the 1978 World Cup group stage, France were scheduled to play Hungary, with the two teams assigned to wear a change white strip and their first-choice red strip respectively. However, FIFA then changed their mind and asked the two to swap to blue and white respectively but the French FA's national team supervisor Henri Patrelle did not read the memo. Only as the teams were both warming up was the error spotted, by which point their original strips were 350 miles away at their Buenos Aires base. Kick-off was delayed as a police car was dispatched at high speed to retrieve the green and white striped jerseys of local side Club Atlético Kimberley. Having ironed numbers 2-11 on to the blank shirts, which did not match up with the starters' assigned numbers, the French side won 3-1 in their makeshift outfits.

Similar incidents had previously seen Mexico line up against Sweden in club side Cruzeiro's blue and white stripes against Switzerland at the 1950 tournament, and Argentina sporting Malmö's yellow strip in their opening World Cup match in 1958. England chose a white first and sky blue change strip at the 1970 World Cup, with the idea that the lighter shades would keep the players cooler in the unfamiliar heat in Mexico. Unfortunately, in their final group game against a Czechoslovakia side sporting white shirts, the change strip was difficult to distinguish in the blazing sun with the effect magnified for the majority of TV viewers watching on black and white sets.

More recently, Chelsea forgot to bring their away kit for their Premier League tie at Coventry City in April 1997. As their royal blue jersey clashed with the navy and sky blue of the home team, after a 15-minute delay Chelsea emerged in the red and black checkerboard away shirts of their opponents. With Coventry's crest taped over on some shirts but not others, Chelsea's disorganised appearance was mirrored in their play as an early second-half collapse saw them lose 3-1.

An important issue which has only recently received attention is colour blindness, which affects one in 12 men and one in 200 women. The condition affects individuals' ability to distinguish between different colour tones. This impacts on the ability of players, officials and spectators to watch and play football. Former Republic of Ireland international Matthew Holland, who spent several seasons playing in the Premier League with

Ipswich Town and Charlton Athletic, spoke to the BBC in 2020 about the challenges he faced as a colour-blind player, 'Generally, I was OK in games but occasionally struggled when the kits were quite close colour-wise. The biggest challenge was having to take a split second longer to make a decision on where I was going to pass the ball to make certain I was passing to a team-mate.' The Premier League and UEFA have offered guidance on kit selection, and the Premier League regulations explicitly state that the needs of colour-blind people should be considered in kit selection. In June 2022, the Football League agreed to allow clubs to wear an away kit at home when it was required to allow a sufficient contrast.

While a club's colours are now a key part of their identity, in the first half a century of organised football they would commonly change strips and few of today's clubs play in their original choice of strip. Liverpool started in a blue and white-halved kit in 1892, whereas the likes of Juventus (pink), Newcastle United (red), Ajax (black with a red sash) and Bayern Munich (light blue) all adopted a distinctly different colourway for their inaugural seasons. A notable exception to this is Nottingham Forest, who first agreed to wear red tasselled caps in Garibaldi red (named after Italian freedom fighter Giuseppe Garibaldi) in 1865, adopting an all-red jersey for the first time in 1866. Indeed, data from the Historical Kits website shows that only around 40 per cent of Football League clubs had adopted their current-day permanent colours by 1900. As such, from 1887 to 1905 these clubs would change their strip every two and a half seasons on average, decreasing to every three and a half seasons between 1905 and 1939 as teams began to establish regular colours and styles. The advent of television, replica shirts and sponsorships meant that clubs began to change their shirts more regularly after the Second World War with the average shirt in the 21st century lasting for just 1.3 seasons.

The emerging English game was dominated by the upper classes, and as a result their colours often reflected the origins of teams derived from professional occupations (Civil Service and Royal Engineers), public school alumni (Old Carthusians, Old Etonians) and leading universities such as Oxford and Cambridge. As the game developed, many clubs took their colour scheme from the company or educational establishment of the founding members. Coventry City was originally a works team for employees of the bicycle manufacturing firm Singers (Singers FC), and wore the company's colours of pink and blue in 1889 before adopting a black shirt with a large 'S' over the heart. West Ham United played in dark blue as founder Arnold Hill had attended Oxford University. Barcelona's distinctive red and blue stripes are taken from the rugby team of the Merchant Taylor's school in Liverpool that founding members Frederick Arthur and Ernest Witty attended. Along the same lines, Saint-Étienne play in the green of the grocery store their founders worked for, and Blackburn Rovers wore the blue and white halves of their founders' Malvern school. In the 1930s, York City swapped their maroon jerseys for chocolate and cream stripes as a tribute to the city's confectionery industry – a colour scheme that was revived for their 2022/23 away kit. More prosaically, white was also a popular choice for early solid-coloured shirts.

This was due to their low cost and the fact that many football clubs arose from cricket clubs to occupy their players in the winter, allowing their whites to serve as a football kit.

Many national teams such as Nigeria and Argentina play in the colours of their national flag, while other teams adopt colour schemes with local significance. Having painfully missed out on winning the 1950 World Cup after losing the decisive last match of the final group stage – that year's tournament wasn't decided by the familiar knockout rounds – to Uruguay in their original white shirts, a newspaper competition was launched to determine a new Brazil kit design which incorporated the national flag's colours. Eighteen-year-old newspaper illustrator Aldyr Schlee, later to become a celebrated author and academic, sketched out over 100 designs when preparing his competition entry. His winning design featured the yellow shirt with green trim which would soon become synonymous with Brazilian success.

There are few teams with a more glamorous history than Ligue 1 side Monaco, and their distinctive red and white diagonal halved shirt also has royal origins. Oscar-winning actress Grace Kelly become Princess Grace of Monaco after marrying Prince Rainier in 1956. Following the club's maiden French Cup win in 1960, she proposed replacing their red and white with the current design based on the principality's flag. The team won their first national championship the following season, and the design has been retained ever since. Another team with royal connections is Italy. Their blue shirt is based on the colour of the House of Savoy, the royal family at the time of the country's first official match in 1910.

More local inspiration is seen in Valencia's away shirt, which commonly features the yellow, red and blue of the city coat of arms. Other strips point to the religious, ethnic or national origins of a team. AEK Athens was founded by Greek refugees from Istanbul, and their yellow and black colours mark the flag of the Byzantine Empire. Celtic and Hibernian's green strips are a nod to their founder's Irish origins, the Catholic Church having been an active supporter in both clubs' foundations. On the other side of Scottish football's religious divide, Unionist or Presbyterian clubs featured red, white and blue, as with a bold striped design used by Hearts in 1876/77.

Other clubs owe their colourways to the romantic convictions of their founders, including several Italian sides. Having played in a Genoa-style red and blue-halved design from their foundation in 1898, Sicilian club Palermo switched to their distinctive pink and black in 1907. This was at the suggestion of founder Count Giuseppe Airoldo, who in a 1905 letter described the colours as, 'The sweet and the sad. A good fit for a team characterised by results as up and down as a Swiss clock.' This description continued to be apt, as the team have experienced 30 promotions and relegations in 90 league seasons to date, including seven in the last 12 seasons prior to the writing of this book. AC Milan have sported the same striped shirt since their inception in 1899, founder Herbert Kilpin proposing that their colours 'will be red like fire and black like the fear we will instil in our opponents'. Sporting romantics Lazio wear light blue and white as a tribute to Olympic founders Greece, the club having begun as a multi-sports organisation.

Some colours arrived as a matter of convenience or happy accident, such as Juventus's original pink shirts made from leftover fabric from the underwear factory owned by one of the founders' fathers. Similarly, Fiorentina's distinctive purple strip is a result of a colour run when their original red and white-halved shirts were washed in the River Arno. Internazionale, known colloquially as Inter Milan in English-speaking countries, sport a striped design which originated from the desk of one of their founders, designer Giorgio Muggiani. Noticing a half-blue, half-red pencil on his desk, he decided that the shirts would be blue and black in contrast to AC Milan's red and black design.

Boca Juniors are Argentina's most successful club with over 70 titles but owe their distinctive colours to a loss. The game in question was played against local team Nottingham de Almagro to decide which of the two would keep their thin blue striped shirts. The club then agreed to adopt the flag colours of the first ship that sailed into port, which was the Swedish *Drottning Sophia*, resulting in their blue and yellow strip. More fortunately, Club Atlético Platense's white and brown colours are those of a race-winning jockey after the proceeds from a bet on his victory were used to buy the club's first strip. Continuing with the Argentinian theme, Vélez Sarsfield's white and blue chevron jersey originated as a set of rugby shirts gifted to the team after the purchaser failed to collect them.

They say that imitation is the best form of flattery, and many clubs' established colours originated as a tribute to other teams or due to fan connections. Athletic Club from Bilbao and Atlético Madrid (originally a youth branch of the former) used to wear Blackburn Rovers' blue and white-halved shirts. Leeds' original blue and white striped kit was based on that of local giants Huddersfield Town, with the switch to an all-white strip in the early 1960s being a more fruitful attempt to emulate Real Madrid's record. Eibar, Levante and Huesca all wear Barcelona's colours, whereas Real Betis's green and white stripes are inspired by the hoops of Celtic. Manuel Ramos Asensio had visited the club's Parkhead stadium regularly during schooling in Scotland and returned with a passion for the club and their colours. Betis celebrated this link in 2017, wearing a hooped shirt for an Andalusia Day match against Málaga in February 2017. Blackpool adopted the Netherlands shirt following a recommendation by club director Albert Hargreaves, after he refereed one of the country's matches. More controversial was Stockport County's adoption of Argentina's sky blue and white stripes for their home kit from 1979. Manager Mike Summerbee used his Adidas connections to obtain a new strip, and the German firm supplied spare sets of the 1978 World Cup winners' kit. While initially a hit with fans, County had to swiftly change kit in April 1982 as the Falklands War broke out, pitting England and Argentina against each other.

Less flatteringly, some clubs adopted other teams' colours through convenience of that particular strip being available or being donated to the club. Juan Elorduy was assigned to bring new kit for Athletic Club on a trip to England, and returned with Southampton's red and white stripes which they wear to this day. Famously, in 1903 Juventus replaced their pink strip (which had faded badly in the wash) with the black and white of leading English side Notts County. The club's English player Tom Savage had implored that their Nottinghamshire kit supplier, 'send us at once an elegant trousseau by team; let it be something lively, something eye-catching. We are tired of our muffled old-fashioned upholstery.' An apocryphal story suggests that West Ham United replaced their Oxford Blue kit with Aston Villa's claret and blue, after West Ham's coach won a sprint against Villa's players and – not having enough money to pay a bet made on the outcome – they gave him a set of their kits. Sheffield League side Chesterfield Town sported a Union Jack shirt in 1892/93, the shirts having been donated by the landlord of the town's Spital Hotel.

In some cases, clubs have adapted their shirt colours to match those of their sponsor. German side VfL Bochum were sponsored by state lottery provider Faber from 1992. However, in 1997 the sponsor formed a new company, Faber Sportswear, to supply a kit inspired by their rainbow-coloured globe logo. In place of the team's traditional blue home and red or white away shirt, Faber designed dramatic halved shirts with the whole left side made up of broad horizontal rainbow stripes in the order in which they appear in Faber's logo. The shirt was not only painfully bright, but the sponsor flock on the shirt was so stiff that the Bochum players had to tape their nipples to prevent abrasions during matches. Bochum had qualified for the UEFA Cup thanks to a fifth-placed league finish in 1996/97, and wins against Trabzonspor and Club Brugge before a 6-4 aggregate loss to Ajax ensured that this unique shirt attracted attention throughout Europe. While initially unpopular among

Bochum fans, the shirt is now looked upon with greater warmth, meaning that original shirts are rare and highly sought after by collectors.

Less dramatically, Eintracht Frankfurt's 1994/95 home jersey featured a bold geometric design based on sponsor Tetra Pak's logo. In addition, the Swiss packaging firm requested a matching yellow away shirt as opposed to the club's traditional white offering, in tribute to their Swedish origins. In a similar vein, Schalke 04's sponsor Kärcher insisted that the 1996/97 away jersey reflect their well-known yellow and black branding – unfortunately the colours of Schalke's rivals Borussia Dortmund. An unhappy compromise was reached to have a yellow shirt with blue details, much to fans' disgust, although a black Kärcher logo meant that there was still a whiff of *schwarzgelb*.

The Coupe de France has several strict regulations around kit design including sponsorship and club colours. In the seventh and eighth rounds (in which 256 teams are whittled down to 64) clubs are only allowed to wear red, blue, green, yellow or white kits with the home team required to wear white or red. Professional clubs need to write to the French Football Federation (FFF) with a request to wear their own kit, otherwise they are provided with a standard Nike kit as worn by competing amateur sides. For the 100th anniversary of the competition which was created in 1917, the FFF produced a set of commemorative jerseys in partnership with Nike. They featured a specially designed crest, and the namesets featured the previous winners of the trophy with those teams with more cup victories appearing in larger font sizes. These jerseys were supplied to each of the 1,312 sides (including 180 based outside mainland France) who had qualified for the fourth and fifth rounds of that season's competition.

More than merely delineating the two sides for the benefit of players, officials and fans, leading figures in football have been convinced of the ability of a kit's colours to influence performance. Liverpool's legendary manager Bill Shankly introduced an all-red strip in the mid-1960s, in an attempt to make the team appear more intimidating to the opposition. The new look was debuted on 25 November 1964 against European giants Anderlecht, albeit with white socks, with the Merseyside team running out 3-0 winners. As ever the footballing romantic, Shankly was entranced, 'Tonight I went out on to Anfield and for the first time there was a glow like a fire was burning … Christ, the players looked like giants. And we played like giants.'

In contrast, fellow Glaswegian icon Sir Alex Ferguson blamed Manchester United's grey away shirt for a terrible first-half performance against perennial Premier League strugglers Southampton in 1996. The team had previously recorded one draw and three losses in four matches in the unusual strips. Finding themselves 3-1 behind and a man down at half-time, Sir Alex ordered his players to change into their blue and white third shirt. Taking advice from vision expert Professor Gail Stephenson, the Red Devils boss suggested that the shirt's pattern had made it difficult for his players to pick each other out against the crowd at The Dell. A decade later, Nike designer Stewart Scott-Curran was part of a team that pitched the idea of another grey shirt to Ferguson, having made considerable efforts to ensure that the pattern and colour would not affect performance. The Scot's response is unprintable.

While United's grey kit 'excuse' caused amusement among fans, there is some scientific evidence that duller colours like grey may hinder the ability of players to pick each other out on the pitch. More conspicuous designs may also influence concentration in high-pressure situations such as a penalty. Psychologists suggest that red is perceived as an aggressive colour, indicating power and dominance, and many even have physiological impacts such as boosting testosterone levels. A potential downside is that these qualities may also attract the attention of officials, who have been shown to be more likely to judge a tackle as a bookable offence if the player is wearing red.

Studies have looked at the thousands of match results available where details of shirt colour were also recorded. Analysis of both the Dutch Eredivisie and English Premier League, where over 7,500 games over the first 20 seasons were available, has shown that red teams are more successful. However, as discussed earlier in this chapter, many leading clubs have copied each other's strips and so it may be that these results are the result of imitation rather than a genuine performance effect. This is supported by findings from La Liga, where no team plays in a solid red shirt and in which no effect of kit colour was found. On the international scene, a study of penalty takers and goalkeepers also found that kit colour did not influence performance. To get around the biases that might be evident in chosen kit colours, researchers have taken to the sport science laboratory to examine the effects in a more robust way. Again, the results are conflicting; while keepers were less confident of saving a penalty when the taker wore red, the shooters themselves felt less confident in the study. So, to date it is unclear whether kit colour can really make a difference to a team's fortunes.

Beyond science, some figures in football have been convinced of the paranormal powers of certain kit colours. Cardiff City fans were incensed by owner Vincent Tan's 2012 decision to change their blue home shirt, worn since the early 1900s, to a red tone considered lucky in Tan's native Malaysia. While the switch was followed by a promotion to the Premier League in 2012/13, the following two seasons saw them relegated in last place and then finish in mid-table, 38 points behind Championship winners Bournemouth. Amid high-profile fan protests, the blue home strip returned from 2015. Conversely, Spain's Euro 2008-winning coach Luis Aragonés was convinced that yellow shirts would bring bad luck to his side. Such was his ill-feeling towards the colour, when star player Raúl arrived at a team meeting in a yellow shirt, Aragonés ordered him to change immediately. By unfortunate coincidence, the Spanish adopted a yellow away strip in 2008, which Aragonés referred to as 'mustard'. His fears about the colour proved unfounded as his team dispatched Russia 3-0 in the European Championship semi-final – their only appearance in the strip.

The Design

BELGIUM 1984. Denmark 1986. Netherlands 1988. West Germany 1990. Nigeria 2018. All unmistakeable shirts that have become almost recognisable as brands in their own right. Some designs are so iconic that they exist only as a nickname, such as the 'Bruised Banana' (Arsenal away 1991–1993) and the 'Snowflake' (Manchester United away 1990–1992). Both shirts have been re-released by their clubs, inspired recent away kit designs, and were even recently reconstructed as pre-match Humanrace shirts designed by musician Pharrell Williams. That these designs are so revered even 30 years after their release shows the potential for a distinctive shirt to become an integral part of a nation's or club's history.

The advent of the replica shirt industry in the 1970s and the invention of cheap dye-sublimation and Jacquard weaving techniques in the 1980s gave designers almost unlimited capacity for creativity in shirt design.

This has resulted in strips inspired by almost every conceivable influence, from city maps and mythical creatures to revolutionary leaders and the humble baked bean. As with the high-tech garment itself, these lurid motifs are a far cry from the largely functional designs worn in the game's infancy.

Plain or hooped shirts were initially common until the late 1880s, when Bolton's Rothwell Hosiery Company designed a loom permitting vertical striped shirts, which quickly became synonymous with football. Derby County kit history site est1884.com unearthed an 1887 newspaper article reporting this innovation, which gives an idea of its novelty and the excitement around the technology, 'We have been favoured with an inspection of a new football jersey which we make bold to presume will carry the market with a rush. For a long time there has been a demand for the stripes lengthways instead of around the body, but this was to be had only by sewing the material in the form desired. Now, however, a machine has been set at work by which the stripes can be knitted in the required direction, and it is expected to effect quite a revolution. The jerseys we have examined are exceedingly neat in appearance, and being very elastic they set off the figure to advantage, and at the same time afford every comfort. Any club designs can be woven according to order, there being practically no limit in this direction. The machine – the only one of its kind – is the property of the Rothwell Hosiery Co., Market-street, Bolton, who can safely guarantee not only a handsome but a perfect fitting article.'

Halved shirts like Blackburn Rovers' strip, and quartered designs such as Bristol Rovers' colours, were also common. The lack of variety in shirt designs is exemplified by those worn by the 12 founding members of the Football League in its inaugural season in 1888/89. Accrington, Bolton Wanderers and Preston North End wore plain shirts; Aston Villa, Blackburn Rovers, Derby County, Everton and Notts County wore quarters (halved shirts with opposing colour sleeves); and Burnley, Stoke, West Bromwich Albion and Wolverhampton Wanderers chose striped shirts. Even with the addition of the Second Division in 1892 which expanded the competition to 28 teams, Wolves' new diagonal halved gold and black strip was the only exception to the three original design types.

The early 20th century began to see innovation in shirt design as clubs began to adopt more adventurous styles. Star Trek-style yoked shirts, with a different coloured panel around the shoulders, were worn by Liverpool and Bradford City among others. Brentford adopted a chalk stripe design in 1903, although the style became popular much later following consecutive FA Cup Final appearances as a change shirt for Manchester City and Aston Villa respectively in 1956 and 1957. Manchester United wore a chevron design when winning their first FA Cup in 1909, a style still famously worn by Scottish side Airdrieonians in addition to several rugby league teams. This silhouette was adopted by Nike for the full range of Old Trafford centenary shirts in 2009, with the white home keeper shirt with red chevron matching the original FA Cup Final design. In an early attempt at performance clothing, thicker vertical stripes became common, with the aim of making the wearer appear larger and more imposing.

As with the shirt itself, there was little innovation in the designs that would feature on it throughout the first half of the

20th century. The spread of floodlights and night matches saw plain kits become popular, particularly in a dazzling white as adopted by teams including Coventry City and Leeds United. This accelerated the gradual move away from patterned shirts, which Chris Stride and colleagues from the University of Sheffield showed to account for around 60 per cent of home football shirts in 1888/89 but less than 30 per cent at their nadir in 1969/70. This trend for simplicity also saw clubs including Liverpool and Chelsea adopt matching shirts, shorts and socks, a practice first launched by innovator Jimmy Hill's Coventry City and their sky blue kit. The absence of distinguishing features also meant that shirts were interchangeable and, in the absence of a club badge, rivals Arsenal (in the brief period where they abandoned their famous white sleeves) and Manchester United wore identical shirts. This trend was swiftly reversed in the following decade, as teams such as Bristol Rovers and Sheffield Wednesday dropped plain shirts for their historical quartered or striped kits. This may have also been influenced by the advent of colour television, Liverpool and West Ham featuring in the first live match in colour on 15 November 1969.

As discussed further on in 'The Printing' and 'The Replica' chapters, the emergence of fully branded replica kits was the catalyst for the emergence of bolder, club-specific designs. These also began to incorporate manufacturer-specific features such as sleeve trims incorporating their logo. Adidas debuted their famous three stripe sleeves in designs for the 1974 World Cup, with brands such as Admiral, Umbro and Bukta adopting similar features soon after. By 1975/76 custom features worn by First Division teams such as the striped collars and cuffs of Aston Villa, Burnley and Manchester United and the tramline design on Coventry's strip were an early glimpse of what was to come.

The North American Soccer League saw some of the boldest kits to emerge in this new era, including Colorado Caribou's 1978 kit featuring a leather tassel strip across the front of the shirt. Given the effort and expense in designing a new shirt pattern, many manufacturers developed named templates whose distinctive shapes would be adapted to a club or international team's colours. Initially these were quite simple, such as Adidas's 1975–1981 Santos or national team template featuring a plain body and sleeve stripes, which was worn by sides including Belgium, Queens Park Rangers and Marseille.

The advent of sublimated printing in the early 1980s offered opportunities for much more daring, complicated designs. England's 1982 World Cup shirt by Admiral was one of the first to make use of the technique, the broad blue and red bands around the shoulders being embedded into the shirt. While templates are often used as a byword for lazy shirt design, conjuring up images of poor-quality Sunday league strips, some of the most-loved shirts in history are derived from a template. Perhaps the most famous example is Adidas's 'Ipswich' design, its sublimated geometric pattern worn by teams including East and West Germany, Porto, Morocco, Borussia Dortmund and the USA but most memorably by the victorious Netherlands squad at the 1988 European Championship. For anyone keen to explore this further,

Chris Oakley has created an excellent list of the 100 greatest templates of all time on his Kitbliss website.

Another innovation which allowed for greater design personalisation was the electronic Jacquard machine, capable of weaving complex patterns into fabric. Early examples were Liverpool's 1985/86 home, away and third strips which featured an image of a liver bird (a mythical creature which is the symbol of the city) and the Adidas trefoil embedded in woven vertical stripes. While not ubiquitous, these patterns were heavily used throughout the 1990s. Like Liverpool's example, many designs featured repeated motifs based on the manufacturer logo, club crest or geometric patterns. A more dramatic example is FC Köln's 1996/97 home kit by Puma, which features a large image of the city's cathedral across the front. Similarly, a giant puma cat logo leapt across a diamond background on Italian side Parma's white, yellow, blue and orange shirts worn in the same season. These patterns were also included on templates, such as Ajax's iconic 1995 Champions League-winning navy and red away shirt which was also sported by teams including Lazio and Spurs.

The advent of the replica industry quickly saw the lifespan of kits diminish; while they had lasted for around five years, this dropped to two years by the early 1980s. The late 1990s also saw the broader introduction of annual kit changes, as clubs sought to maximise the revenue generated from replica sales. While this brought angry protests from many fan groups, the practice is now well established, even with teams in lower divisions. As described in 'The Replica', in the last few years many clubs have taken to releasing a fourth or special kit whereas a select few have spewed out an extraordinary number of kits. In 2021/22, Napoli released a staggering 13 shirts. Domestic home, away, third and fourth jerseys were joined by four European competition versions and four special-edition kits featuring club icon Diego Maradona who had passed away in the previous season. Finally, a Halloween shirt with a spider-web design was worn in two matches in late October. With prices up to €150, to assemble the full collection would cost over €1,500. Into 2022/23 the club's 'creativity' continued, and while the volume of shirts was slightly smaller (nine to date) the premise of each special release became more tenuous. Home, away and third domestic shirts were again paired with European versions, and a Halloween shirt featuring a cloud of bats in flight. A simplistic, red-nosed reindeer design was released as a €125 Christmas shirt, with a Valentine's Day strip featuring a pair of lips appearing in January for the same price.

The 1980s had seen the start of shirt designs referencing the past, as many long-established clubs looked to commemorate their centenaries. Derby County were one of the first to pursue this, their 1984/85 Admiral design featuring a commemorative crest and broad stripes on the left shoulder in the club's original colours of gold, blue and brown. Into the 1990s, other leading clubs followed suit with retro-inspired designs and features. Manchester United celebrated 100 years in the Football League and Premier League with a green and gold-halved design based on their 1892/93 strip, although more recent research suggests that the original shirt was red and white with the green/gold combination only featuring in a striped shirt the following season. The 1992/93 version also featured a laced collar, the Victorian design feature also adopted by clubs including Blackburn Rovers and Aston Villa, while Newcastle United adopted a 'grandad' collar from 1995 to 1997.

This trend has accelerated in the last few years, as manufacturers exploit the growing interest in retro shirts and other leading sides reached the end of their tenth decade. Barcelona celebrated their centenary in 1999 with a halved red and blue design like that worn at their foundation. Inter Milan marked 100 years since their foundation with a red cross design on a white shirt, referencing the flag of Milan and a design worn in the early years of their history. Having abandoned their original white shirts after disappointment at the 1950 World Cup, Brazil reintroduced the colour in 2019 for the 100th anniversary of their maiden Copa América victory. The team had previously adopted a laced collar design as a one-off for FIFA's centenary match in 2004 in which they and opponents France wore vintage-inspired strips for the first half. In 2020 Chelsea launched a 'blue-out' fourth kit with camouflaged sponsors and Nike branding and a classic club emblem to commemorate the 50th anniversary of their first FA Cup win.

In addition to historic shirts, iconic modern designs have been replicated – in some cases, only a few years after the original. Arsenal's 2019/20 Adidas away shirt was inspired by the club's infamous 1991–1993 'Bruised Banana' away shirt. Adidas also reached for the classics when designing national team shirts for the 2018 World Cup, with eight of the ten designs based on a classic from their past. Belgium 1984, Russia/USSR 1988, Colombia, West Germany, Egypt and Sweden 1990, Argentina 1993 and Spain 1994 were all recreated. Inter Milan are the recent masters of this art via their Nike contract, with overt modern references for their 2020/21 third (1997/98 third), 2021/22 third (1990/91 away) and 2021/22 away (2010/11 away) strips among others. The *pièce de résistance* was the 2018/19 fourth shirt released to mark 20 years with Nike as a kit supplier, which featured a mash-up of the home shirt designs released across the contract.

While retro-inspired kits are often well received by fans, there is a growing feeling among figures in the kit industry that the ubiquitous nature of their historic references is stifling modern design. Journalist and kit expert Denis Hurley said, 'Inspirations for shirts are becoming a bit questionable – we hear "this is the colour of the ticket stub from the time we won the Cup Winners' Cup" or similar. You don't have to bother with that; you can just say this is something our designers thought would look good. Currently, it feels like firms are just looking for a device that lets you believe in the heritage of a design and it's not necessary. You can just ask people to judge it with their eyes and not their hearts.'

Denis suggested that the short kit lifecycle and conservative nature of football fans may contribute, 'As kits are being released each year designers can't just make subtle changes and so they must challenge sensibilities but also make them commercially viable. My colleague Jay Mansfield coined the term "new traditionalism", in that fans are having a strong reaction to anything that they feel is not traditional but that their sense of this is based on what they knew as a child. For example, Bayern fans have successfully argued for blue to be removed from their home shirts, but it is only since the 1970s that Bayern had an all-red shirt. I think people are very critical of modern kits. It's almost like an affectation, "Oh, things were better in the old days."'

Unsurprisingly, many clubs and national teams have looked to their own city or country's culture for inspiration. World Cup 1994 hosts USA's change strip exemplified the audacious designs which were common throughout the decade, as giant white stars from the nation's flag were set against a background of faux blue denim. Nigeria incorporated tribal patterns into their home and away shirts for the same competition. For the following World Cup in France in 1998, Mexico's ABA Sport provided their national team with elaborate home, away and third designs based on the sunstone of the Aztec calendar. These have all proved to be highly sought-after classics, as is Borussia Dortmund's 2019 black-out 110th anniversary kit. The boxed *Kohle und Stahl* (coal and steel) design celebrated the industrial history of the Ruhr, one year after the region's last coal mine closed. Strikingly, Mexican firm Charly produced a series of Day of the Dead-themed shirts for leading Mexican teams, to commemorate the religious holiday. The designs featured icons central to the celebration such as altars, marigolds and skulls.

Music and football have mixed across the pop era and so it is not a surprise to find music is also a popular source of inspiration; for example, Manchester City's 2019/20 away shirt with its black, yellow, pink and blue colour scheme and design celebrating the city's iconic Hacienda nightclub. Similarly, Coventry City's 2019/20 black and white third shirt was inspired by the city's two-one music genre led by well-known band The Specials. Since 2016, German side FC Köln have released a special kit to commemorate the annual carnival which is celebrated across the Rhineland. The shirts include elements such as the city's crest or those relating to carnival dress or the city's cathedral.

Animal-inspired designs have featured heavily since the 1990s, such as Hull City's striking 1992/93 tiger print shirt by Matchwinner. In 1997/98 Athletic Club (The Lions) and Porto's (The Dragons) nicknames inspired the large silhouettes dominating their Kappa away shirts, with AEK Athens' double-headed eagle emblem receiving the same treatment. Inter Milan's black and blue stripes were presented within a snakeskin pattern on their 2021/22 home shirt. This was a tribute to the city's *biscione* (big viper) emblem, which was also draped across the club's 2010/11 and 2021/22 away shirts. In an era of the cultural franchise crossover, it is perhaps inevitable that designs have taken inspiration from other forms of media. Fourth-tier Argentinian side Ferro Carril Oeste featured Homer Simpson emerging from a hedge and the cartoon's Itchy and Scratchy characters on their keeper strips. Meanwhile, to coincide with the release of the latest Star Wars film *The Rise of Skywalker*, large Stormtrooper graphics were splashed across Mexican top-flight side Club Tijuana Xoloitzcuintles de Caliente's 2019/20 strips.

Nations and clubs are increasingly aware of their broader social responsibilities, and the potential of using their shirt's visibility to highlight important social issues. In 2005, numerous Nike-sponsored countries wore a black and white-halved shirt in support of the Stand Up, Speak Up anti-racism campaign. More recently, CD Guadalajara (2015/16) and Altrincham (2018/19) wore rainbow-themed shirts in support of the LGBTQ+ community. Arsenal's 'whiteout' shirt worn in their January 2022 and 2023 FA Cup third-round matches promoted the No More Red anti-knife crime campaign following increases in violence in London. The club did not make the shirts commercially available, and instead gave them to volunteers working with local charities and community projects.

More subtly, Norwegian Eliteserien side Tromsø incorporated a QR code into their 2021 shirt directing users to a page highlighting Qatar's human-rights controversies, in protest at the nation's selection as 2022 World Cup host. For the same tournament, Denmark and suppliers Hummel released kits with national and manufacturer logos and the brand's famous chevron details rendered in the same colour as the fabric. The aim was to avoid actively promoting their participation in the competition, while the black third shirt was described as 'the colour of mourning' in support of the migrant workers who lost their lives during construction work underpinning the global showcase.

One of the clubs to have most successfully exploited the explosion in the football kit market is third-tier US side Forward Madison, founded in 2018 and based in Wisconsin. I covered this topic in 2022 for the website The Online Rule. They developed a unique pink, white, light and navy blue palette which has become their calling card along with their flamingo logo inspired by a 1979 university student prank involving 1,000 plastic birds. Under novice football kit designer Cassidy Sepnieski, the club's 2019 change strip won leading satellite radio channel SiriusXM FC's Kit of the Year prize for 2019 with over 200,000 votes, Forward making more money from their strips than all of their league rivals combined. Indeed, despite their lowly league status, they have outsold several top-tier professional Major League Soccer clubs annually since 2019. Their 2020 'Drip' third kit, created by Sepnieski after watching an Instagram video involving swirling paint into water, was even more successful, leading to a partnership with the world's largest vintage football shirt retailer CFS.

In 2021, a surfeit of ideas led to the team creating a reversible kit combining two designs with each worn for a half in a league match against Greenville Triumph SC. The shirt featured Forward's ever-present sponsors, local automotive insurance company Dairyland and Madison's Just Coffee Cooperative. The club's director of digital content Evan Warwick explained that the shirts would not just provide revenue but also increase Forward's profile, allowing them to sign players like Trinidad and Tobago international Alvin Jones who might otherwise play at a higher level. Forward's innovations continued into 2021 when they released a 'Friends With Benefits' kit allowing their international fans to buy a beer for domestic fans attending their home matches.

Dramatic designs have recently been used to attract attention for teams who raise money for charity. Chief among these is Yorkshire amateur side Bedale AFC, who donate 25 per cent of their kit revenue to Prostate Cancer UK. Sponsored by sausage-manufacturer Heck, their sausage-themed kits have included a hot dog bun strip and 2022's toad in the hole design. Most dramatically, they released the world's first see-through kit, in 2021. Featuring the charity's tagline 'DON'T FORGET TO CHECK', the design features arrows pointing towards the wearer's groin.

More conventionally, in recent years Swedish club AIK have released a series of ultra low-volume special-edition shirts in luxury presentation boxes. The kits celebrate the club's anniversary with all proceeds going to local charities. Founded in 1891, the number of shirts made available is based on the anniversary year, with the 128, 129 and 131 units from their three releases to date being snapped up in minutes. Similarly, Parma celebrated their 108th birthday in 2021 by releasing a 200-unit *in campo per loro* ('on the pitch for them') shirt. The proceeds were donated to the city's Children's Hospital, with the rainbow panel design on the sleeves based on the building's façade. In 2022, Forward Madison raised tens of thousands of pounds for UNICEF's Ukrainian relief effort appeal with a yellow and blue version of their sash strip.

Several Spanish lower-league teams sported unusual kits in the 2010s thanks to TV executive and former semi-professional player Juan Francisco Martín Fresneda, as told to ESPN in a 2020 article. Originally approached to work as a consultant by cash-strapped third division side Cultural Leonesa when director of León's TV network, Martín Fresneda used his background in marketing to come up with a black tuxedo design shirt with a white version worn by the Cultural keeper for their 90th anniversary in 2014/15. The kits were a huge success, the club selling nearly 5,000, whereas only 20 or 30 of the most hardcore fans would normally buy their new strips. The promotion also attracted international press attention, and Cultural were bought by Qatari group Aspire. Despite the attention and revenue saving the stricken club, many fans felt that the stunt had led to a loss of Cultural's identity. When they drew Real Madrid in the Copa del Rey that season, Martín Fresneda saw the high-profile tie as a huge marketing opportunity for the club via their kit. However, Cultural took fan criticism on board and the team appeared in the Santiago Bernabéu Stadium in a more traditional strip.

Following the success of the tuxedo kit, Martín Fresneda was soon approached by other clubs for assistance. A call from an old team-mate saw Cultural's saviour come to the rescue of fourth-division side Palencia in 2015/16. While Palencia were pushing for promotion on the pitch, financial problems meant that the players had not been paid for two months and were understandably threatening to go on strike. Taking a loan from the club's IT company sponsor Ingenova, Martín Fresneda overcame the scepticism of the players to produce another winning design. Based on a Spanish football idiom 'to leave your skin on the pitch', meaning to give everything to win, the Kappa-produced shirt featured a design of a skinless torso showing the muscles and tendons. The original batch of shirts were sold out within an hour, going on to sell thousands internationally with Palencia being promoted at the end of the season.

Martín Fresneda approached his next club, Atlético Astorga, who played in green, with the idea of an Incredible Hulk-themed version of the muscle shirt. Even more spectacular than the design was the kit launch, the players appearing to smash through a brick wall to emerge in the strips. Finally, in 2018 third-division side Zamora were €700,000 in debt and looking for investors so Martín Fresneda persuaded them that one of his distinctive designs could help promote the club. Called 'Blood, Sweat and Tears', as an analogue of the Cultural kit the design showed the cardiovascular system with the Zamora crest positioned at its heart. The sales revenue and attention helped to stabilise the club, who were promoted the following season.

Not all designs have been universally well received, to the point that in some cases shirts have been withdrawn or altered mid-season. Most shockingly, the geometric design of Fiorentina's 1992/93 shirt featured a repeating pattern of interlocking arrows which formed a swastika. This was particularly sensitive as the club's left-leaning, anti-fascist fanbase were keen to erase the stigma of having been formed under fascist politician Luigi Ridolfi at the behest of Mussolini. Fiorentina issued a statement, 'Fiorentina and the manufacturers, Lotto, would like to underline that the optical effect is purely a matter of chance,' with Lotto claiming that a computer program had generated the pattern randomly. Despite this clarification, the offensive strips were replaced mid-season with a modified version in which the offending areas were redrawn. This was the start of a miserable season for *La Viola*, who were relegated despite having the likes of Gabriel Batistuta, Stefan Effenberg and Brian Laudrup among their ranks. The modified design was later used by several other teams including Morocco, Linfield and Israeli side Maccabi Haifa.

Another shirt to attract negative attention was Rangers' orange away strip for 2002/03, a season which saw the Scottish side secure a domestic treble under Alex McLeish. The move was described as 'needlessly provocative' by anti-sectarian campaigners and politicians, as orange is particularly associated with controversial Protestant parades. In 2004, Bilbao's Athletic Club released a special-edition European kit to mark their return to continental football after a five-year absence. Celebrated Basque artist Dario Urzay delivered a design with branching red splodges, alternatively described as representing blood spatter or artwork from the city's Guggenheim Museum. Known as the 'ketchup shirt', the fan backlash was so severe that it was never worn in a competitive match with its only appearances coming in pre-season friendlies.

Puma have a history of disruptive designs, and a series of 2021/22 third shirts proved more controversial than most. The design, shared by around a dozen European and South American clubs including AC Milan, Shakhtar Donetsk and Independiente, did not feature a typical club crest badge. Instead, each team's crest was included as a jacquard pattern throughout the shirt with the Puma logo centralised and the team's name written in large font across the chest. Even though teams such as AC Milan had not featured their crests on their strips until the mid-1990s, the kits were seen by many fans as abandoning the clubs' traditions. Pressure by Borussia Dortmund fans led to multiple redesigns of the shirt, with first a larger debossed crest printed on the right chest and then a more visible black plastic outlined version being added. Along similar lines, in November 2010 Nike revealed a Poland national team kit without the traditional eagle emblem. A supporter backlash led to a December 2011 redesign incorporating the iconic insignia.

The shirts above have been worn in several games before being withdrawn or modified, but other designs have been vetoed before making their debut. Adidas's original Argentina shirt design for the 1994 World Cup was withdrawn at the behest of Argentine Football Association president Julio Grondona due to the inclusion of a black pinstripe in addition to the usual white and sky blue bands. The team wore a more traditional strip at the tournament, although Reebok's 2000/01 strip reintroduced black stripes into the design for one season. The 1994 shirt had reached the production stage before being withdrawn, and some copies still exist and are highly sought after by collectors.

Manufacturer Garcis looked to follow up Mexico's classic Aztec 1998 World Cup shirt with a similar design incorporating the Mexican national shield. The country's government refused the federation permission to do this, with the shirt eventually featuring the Mexican Football Federation crest instead. China's 2018 black Nike away shirt, featuring an ornate dragon pattern, made it as far as the Nike.com website but was quickly withdrawn. Amid suggestions that the sacred status of the dragon in Chinese culture meant that the design had caused offence, the shirt never resurfaced again. The few shirts that were sold are now highly prized, going for several times their original purchase price on the rare occasion that they appear on auction sites or social media. Finally, a potential 2020/21 shirt featuring the red cross of Catalonia's patron saint Jordi was rejected by Barcelona's board as the white background was deemed to be too similar to rivals Real Madrid's colours. This is despite white having been a popular away kit choice for the team for several decades up to 1980.

Given the complexity of UEFA's design regulations as described in 'The Sponsor', it is perhaps not surprising that several clubs and countries have fallen foul of them. For European matches, Ajax were forced to remove the three little bird symbols, relating to a Bob Marley song popular among the club's fans, from the neck of their celebrated Marley-inspired 2021/22 third shirt. Similarly, Inter Milan had to adapt the 'biscione' snake motif across their 2021/22 away shirt as large pictorial patterns are not permitted. Serie A regulations require that the club emblem can only appear once on a strip, which meant that newly promoted Venezia had to redesign their 2021/22 Serie A shirts. The Kappa design featured the club's name in lieu of a sponsor in addition to the club crest, which was interpreted as two separate club emblems. Finally, Turkish side Galatasaray were forced to redesign their home shirt as the diagonal design extended past the shoulder on to the sleeve on the front only. As such, it did not fit with any of the styles permitted under UEFA regulations.

So how do these designs emerge, and what is the process followed to produce a leading team's kit? Through examining the experiences of different design teams across eras, we can get an idea of how aspects such as technology and the level of commercial interest have transformed the development process.

For Admiral's designers in the 1970s, the early replica era, a key aim was developing distinctive club-specific designs that only they could replicate, and which justified the high purchase price. In addition, the shirts needed to look good on television which effectively became an advertising vehicle for the company's wares. This was made more challenging by the lack of dye-sublimation and Jacquard technologies which would revolutionise this process in the following decades. Simple printing or woven patterns could be made into more complex shapes such as the horizontal chevrons on West Ham's 1976–1980 home strip, or the curved tramlines sewn by hand on to Coventry City's home kits. Most of the company's designers had backgrounds in fashion and few had an interest in football, which has been a surprisingly common theme among successful football designers. Dave Moor describes this as an advantage, 'They came to it without any baggage. For me, Newcastle United wore stripes. They had to be a certain thickness, and they had to look like the stripes that were worn by the team in the 1950s and going back even further. And that all changed with the Admiral revolution.' Hand-drawn on paper with felt-tip markers, the designs featured few historical, cultural or fan references. A pattern was set for future football design in that while traditional colours were retained for the home shirt, the away strip was seen as a playground for a greater degree of experimentation.

The 1980s saw more established firms experiment with more adventurous designs, with an eye on the growing adult replica market. A good example is West Germany's 1990 World Cup finals home shirt – one of the most recognisable kits of all time. The design represented a substantial departure from the plain white shirts of the past, incorporating the black, red and yellow of the nation's flag in jagged horizontal bands. These were included at the behest of company chairman Horst Dassler and formed a bold statement for a divided country still wrestling with the shadows of its past. The design team of four was led by Ina Franzmann and was responsible for all the company's football kits plus athletics and tennis wear. They used hand-drawn designs as computer graphics packages were still in their infancy. This small group was also responsible for the 'Ipswich' template sported by teams including the Netherlands' victorious 1988 European Championship squad. The focus of the West Germany design was appearance rather than performance, with the graphic intended to emphasise the players' shoulders. The geometric design curves upwards, symbolising winning with a popular myth suggesting that it mapped the country's results across previous editions of the World Cup while also predicting their eventual victory in the 1990 tournament.

In the 2018 Fabric of Football exhibition organised by the National Football Museum and retailer Classic Football Shirts,

Franzmann spoke of having much more freedom to focus on the design itself rather than considering its commercial impact. Initially the design was a victim of football conservatism, with its bold graphic and colouring attracting criticism. Like many classics, the reputation of the shirt has grown over time. Ina was not a football fan and having delivered the design and moved on to other roles including that of Adidas's chief designer, she was unaware of its impact until many years later. She told the National Football Museum's Strip exhibition, 'To be completely honest, I didn't even know about the hype of this shirt, and it was surprising when I heard it was favoured among the football enthusiasts. It makes me truly happy after 30 years knowing that it became an icon, and it influenced the whole soccer shirt business. I'm proud, and it's fantastic. I'm happy to be the designer of this iconic shirt.' Having been used in the 1988 European Championship, none other than manager and former player Frank Beckenbauer led the successful campaign for it to be retained for the next major tournament, in Italy, which they won.

The 1990s kit design revolution is illustrated well by the example of Nike and their head designer Drake Ramberg. Another football outsider, the Portland native was assigned to head up Nike's new European office, serving major clubs including Paris Saint-Germain (supplied by the company from 1989 to date), Borussia Dortmund (1990–2000), Lyon (1991–1995) and Arsenal (1994–2014). He and his team were one of the first to incorporate club and city culture into designs. They would talk to staff and fans, and visit the city and stadium to understand the history and icons which could be woven into the new strips. An example of this is the eagle feather motif on the sleeves of the Borussia Dortmund 1994/95 shirts, which referenced the eagle emblem on the city's flag. The design was also adopted by the Nigeria team who were a fellow member of the Nike stable, in reference to their nickname, the 'Super Eagles'.

The revolutionary nature of the team's outputs can be seen by contrast to the final Adidas designs worn by Paris Saint-Germain and Borussia Dortmund in 1988 and 1989. PSG had sported a white home shirt with two simple vertical stripes, while Dortmund had a custard yellow jersey with a vertical stripe woven in the jacquard. Nike presented PSG's off-centre red and blue vertical stripes in the shape of the Eiffel Tower from 1990 to 1992, and neither this traditional design nor the famous Hechter stripe appeared on the 1992/93 shirts. In place of Borussia Dortmund's golden yellow, from 1990 to 1998 the home shirts were rendered in a million-watt neon shade called 'Volt Yellow'. Jacquard motifs included club crests, Nike's 'Premier' branding and shapes assigned to the club such as a lightning bolt for Arsenal. This was very much the designers' and fans' decade, with commercial considerations now the focus until the approach of the new millennium. Little attention was paid to performance which is unsurprising in an era where many leagues still had a strong player drinking culture and aspects of sport science such as diet were yet to be fully considered. The team also had to adapt to the growing intrusion of regulations around areas such as sponsorship, providing Dortmund with a 'European' shirt version featuring a smaller, simplified sponsor.

Moving into the new millennium, design teams now had to marry commercially successful designs with the new focus on performance. As Jürgen Rank, senior design director at Adidas, revealed to the *Football Kit Podcast*, the scale of the design task and team has grown in recent years. Adidas now has a team of around a dozen full-time designers to deliver the multiple annual kit designs required for leading clubs, and every second year for national sides. In contrast, Rob Warner recalled only one football designer being employed at Puma to serve the likes of Lazio, Monaco, Everton, Wolfsburg, Cameroon, and the Czech Republic when he joined the company in 2001. As part of a series of pieces on Manchester United's Nike kit era from 2002 to 2015, I spoke to the company's ex-designers Stewart Scott-Curran, Ffion Appleton-Jones and Craig Buglass about the demands of delivering for elite teams and their global fanbase in the modern era. In addition to the inaugural Premier League winners, the team had worked concurrently with giants including Barcelona and Brazil.

The trio explained that given the scale of production, designs are commonly finalised 18 months in advance of release. At all stages, the design team need to ensure that their proposals meet the very stringent regulations in place for playing equipment. The modern UEFA Equipment Regulations document is 68 pages long containing around 60 articles, covering not only players' shirts but any equipment, clothing or items such as balls or medical equipment likely to appear on the field of play.

Teams are only permitted one sponsor (which cannot be related to tobacco, or alcohol above 15 per cent ABV) on the front of the shirt (maximum 200cm^2), a sleeve sponsor (max 100cm^2) and a non-commercial sponsor on the reverse (max 100cm^2). Regulations mandate the size and positioning of sponsors, badges, domestic title and star markings, manufacturer logos, namesets and numbers; in addition, the permitted colours and patterns, pattern-free regions for printing and sleeve logos.

In a reverse of the previous decade's approach, designers in the modern era begin by planning the technical methodology, which materials are going to be used, the shirt's construction and features such as moisture management. This might sound strange given the importance placed by fans on the shirt's appearance. However, having spoken to several modern designers they are all unequivocal that giving a team the best shirts in terms of performance is the number-one priority. Indeed, Rob Warner recalled the simple Puma design brief for their 2006 World Cup team shirts, 'Get players to the ball faster.'

The cost of implementing these features and the need to avoid accusations of a sporting advantage for certain clients means that top countries and clubs are often given the same technical base or template. Firms also make a huge amount of money from these templates being sold to semi-professional and amateur clubs so having distinctive designs at major tournaments effectively acts as advertising for this market as well. An additional consideration is a practical one, in that innovations such as the Powerbands in Adidas's 2010 World Cup Techfit shirts are visually very prominent and designs must incorporate them. Similarly, the characteristics of new materials such as how they hold colour and the ability to print small details will influence the flexibility that the team has to implement their designs. The demands of individual teams are also considered; the Czech Republic's 2006 stars were 5ft 10in Tomáš Rosický and 6ft 8in Jan Koller so the designers worked hard to consider a style that would suit both players.

The team then move into the design element, beginning with the brand's current plans and aesthetic. Often they develop a theme guiding their design for a World Cup cycle or particular season, with inspiration coming from the most unusual places. Craig Buglass revealed the unusual inspiration behind Nike's 2002 World Cup range. Being mesmerised by a dayglo orange flyer handed to him outside an Amsterdam nightclub, he thought, 'That's massive! That's cool!' and the 'Massive Colour' concept was born. Using painfully bright shades of team's traditional colours including Netherlands orange, Brazil yellow and Nigeria green, a range of dazzling shirts were produced.

The team then focus on the 'story' they want to tell for that club or country. Jürgen Rank spoke about the idea of seeing each year's kits as a collection. For 2020/21, Manchester United's home kit was quite traditional with a fleck based on the back of the woven club crest. The murky green away kit represented the city, its hand-drawn wave patterns inspired by the city's three rivers whereas the outlandish dazzle camo third shirt was at the opposite end of the innovation spectrum. The design teams are fully aware of which shirts will provoke a reaction, and for them the polarising effect of certain designs is a positive as it attracts attention and hopefully affection. The design process usually involves a visit to the club, particularly if this is the first shirt with a team new to the brand. The designers will speak to players, the management team and directorship and most importantly the fans to identify the moments and cultural icons that could be referenced in designs. Some clubs have a museum or retain a collection of older kits, giving designers direct access to their predecessor's work.

Understandably, the priority in terms of design remains the top-tier international and club teams with less resource being devoted to lower-ranked sides. The elite clubs and countries might be given a new neckline design, a custom jacquard or sublimated pattern or a high-detail badge design. Outside the most highly ranked organisations, many clubs would be given a template adapted to their colours rather than receiving a bespoke shirt. It is important to remember the scale at which these clubs operate, often selling millions of units per season, so even small custom design features have substantial financial implications. For example, implementing a 5p button collar on Bayern Munich's three million replica shirts would add £150,000 to the annual production costs. For custom shirts, the design team will then give an initial presentation of their concept together with fabric samples and other technical details to team stakeholders and use this feedback to inform the three-to-four-month design process. Returning with the near-finalised design and kit samples, they will then take the opportunity to tweak the final product. The final presentation is usually made to members of the board, technical and marketing staff, although at Manchester United the Nike team recalled nerve-wracking presentations to a panel of one: Sir Alex Ferguson.

The review process is very intensive; players will be asked about the fit of the shirt, any areas where abrasion is occurring and whether design features such as sweat-wicking are effective. Some players and managers take a keen interest in the process, Craig Buglass noting that Barcelona winger Boudewijn Zenden had the idea of a gold shirt which became the club's 2001/02 away design. Going one step further, Sampdoria's Roberto Mancini actually sketched out the designs for a 1989/90 third kit required due to a kit clash with European Cup Winners' Cup quarter-final opponents Grasshopper Club Zürich.

As players have to appear in front of audiences of millions wearing these shirts, it is perhaps not surprising that many of them have strong views on different designs. At the Fabric of Football exhibition, Ruud Gullit described the Netherlands' 1988 shirt as the ugliest he'd ever worn, which was slightly awkward as its designer Ina Franzmann was also in attendance. He favoured the ultra-simple designs of his club side at the time, AC Milan, explaining, 'If you have a beautiful shirt, you feel better [on the pitch].' In that vein, he described the classic Sampdoria shirt he wore in 1993/94 as the most beautiful ever made. Former Arsenal player Ian Wright was not a fan of another bold design, the club's 'Bruised Banana' 1991–1993 away shirt, 'It's such an iconic shirt, everyone goes crazy for it. When we started wearing it, we hated it … We thought that people were going to laugh at us.' Many fans held the same view at the time, but, like them, Wright's opinion has changed, 'I look back now at the pictures of when we were playing in it – it looks brilliant.'

The level of detail in design is such that Stuart Scott-Curran even visited the Manchester United laundry room to investigate the cause of heavy shirt bobbling on one season's shirt – asking the laundry staff details on the temperature, cycle and washing products used. Such is the interest in new shirt designs that leaks are common, but some companies will plant fake leaks to cause uncertainty when genuine designs hit social media. Jürgen Rank spoke about the disappointment of seeing jerseys leaked early, with poor-quality shots not showing the kits at their best and denying the design team the opportunity to explain the stories behind the look.

Events in the football world can conspire to hamper designers' efforts. Rob Warner recalled an incident from his days designing Lazio's kits during their turn-of-the-millennium heyday. The new season's kits would be presented to the club board complete with a player nameset on the reverse. Rob had taken the apparently safe choice of the previous season's top scorer, Hernán Crespo, and couriered the garment off to Rome on a Friday afternoon. Later that night, news broke of a deal taking the Argentine to Inter Milan as a replacement for the Real Madrid-bound Ronaldo. Amid fan protests at the sale, he came into the office the following morning and printed another sample with a safer choice for rapid delivery to the Stadio Olimpico. Similarly, uncertainty around a new sponsor creates potential problems, design teams developing shirts with the possibility of multiple diverse graphic styles being added to the front. For this reason, designers have spoken of the advantages of the international game where designs can be developed without consideration of an intrusive sponsor. In addition, the two-year lifecycle gives more time for the shirt to build its own history and identity before being replaced.

The advent of the internet and social media also provided a platform for kit fans and collectors to share their interest in kits and designs. Several high-quality websites chronicle kits old and new, such as Dave Moor's Historical Football Kits. In simple figures, the changing styles and colours of predominately English and Scottish club teams are covered, accompanied by a written history of each club's strips. Journalist Denis Hurley's Museum of Jerseys has hundreds of articles on different aspects of kit design including one-off strips, chronicles of a team's season in kits and famous template kits, with the latter also being covered in detail by Chris Oakley's excellent Kitbliss website. John Devlin's True Colours website follows a series of books John released detailing Football League and international kit changes across seasons, which are seen as a 'Bible' for many shirt fans and collectors. *True Colours* was the first book to document kits in detail, and to consider commercial aspects such as sponsors and manufacturers as an integral part of football culture.

The growing popularity of football shirts and interest in retro-inspired designs has seen resources like those listed above increasingly used for academic, cultural and commercial activities on the topic. For example, the National Football Museum launched the exhibition Strip! How Football Got Shirty in 2019, with John Devlin brought in as a consultant. In addition to gallery exhibits, John and fellow kit experts including Dave Moor, Les Motherby and Phil Delves contributed to a series of live events, website, podcasts and other resources which detailed the shirt's evolution. Such is the wealth of information accumulated by these experts, they are now a reference point for new designs. 'Designers and club officials are now getting in touch and telling me that that are using the site when they are talking to their kit supplier about retro or commemorative kits,' Dave revealed. 'This is very gratifying but means if I have made a mistake on an early kit the manufacturers repeat it!'

One prominent example of this problem was Arsenal's redcurrant 2005/06 home shirt worn to commemorate the club's last season at Highbury. The design was based on the premise that a similar shirt was worn during the team's first season in the stadium in 1913/14, which Dave now believes is not the case. 'One of the things I love about this work is that there are lots of myths and untruths about the history of football kits that just get repeated and repeated,' explained Dave. 'It was thought that Arsenal wore dark red shirts in the early days. But they didn't; a couple of historians proved that by going through newspaper records of the time which showed that they wore bright red. But the idea persisted, and I had them on the website in dark red shirts for a long time until I was convinced this was not true. I take as much pleasure from getting material that dispels these myths as I do making new discoveries.'

Recently, some clubs have put their new designs into the hands of fans. The most high-profile example of this is Borussia Dortmund, who ran a contest to design their 2023/24 home shirt online. Having received more than 15,000 entries, the final designs were chosen by a panel including supporter representatives, current captain Marco Reus and former player Dedé before being opened to a public vote. Unsurprisingly, a key theme of these fan-sourced designs was club and city-specific features. A map of the city and an outline of its border, a graphic of the Borsigplatz neighbourhood where the club was founded, a coal seam alluding to the region's industrial history and a silhouette of the club's stadium roof were all original ideas included in the selected entries.

One of the most sought-after replica shirts of 2021 was a special-edition jersey produced by Atlético Mineiro. The Brazilian club celebrated their 113th anniversary with a fan-designed 'Manto da Massa' kit based on a map of their home state Minas Gerais. The words 'Una Vez Ate Morrer' ('Until I Die') were added above Le Coq Sportif's logo with 'Vencer' ('Win') included as a repeating motif on the cuffs and collar. Parisian side Red Star also crowd-sourced designs for their 125th-anniversary shirt released in late 2022, with kit expert Phil Delves's idea being chosen. Phil created an Art Nouveau-style jersey based on the colour palette of a poster by artist Henri Thiriet in 1897, the year Red Star were founded. A leaf graphic from the poster was incorporated as a pattern in the body, collar and cuffs with five stripes representing the Coupe de France titles won by the club between 1921 and 1942 and a retro-style club crest hidden inside the neck.

Many shirt fans see the increased attention on design across traditional and social media as evidence of a new 'golden era' of shirt design. However, this is not a universally accepted view with figures such as kit guru John Devlin suggesting the opposite, 'I think that football shirt design has been in the doldrums for quite a while, it's in a cul-de-sac and it just goes round and round. We started 15 years ago with the concept kits, with everything having a "real-world" influence and I think that it has got out of hand.' Having watched the dramatic evolution of the football shirt from the 1970s to the millennium, John feels that progress has stagnated. Worse still, he feels that the few brands trying to be innovative are being criticised for their creativity, 'I've never been the biggest lover of Puma shirts but for me they're the only company really trying something different. I don't think they've always succeeded but I admire the fact that they're just trying to shift what a shirt can be. More than just round neck, badge on one side, logo on the other.' John suggested that oppressive design regulations are also stifling innovation, leading to a stagnation of the shirt's previously rapid evolution. He cited the example of the Adidas team who designed Arsenal's 'Bruised Banana' remake, who had to go back to UEFA numerous times before approval because the colour differentiation (which was the primary feature of the original shirt) was too strong.

The Sponsor

THE SPONSOR is now as much a part of the identity of a football shirt as its colourway, design or the crest it sports. The logos of brands as diverse as Die Continentale, Newcastle Brown Ale, ABN-AMRO, ERG and Nintendo instantly conjure up vivid images of teams, players and the matches in which they were worn. Within each club, the sponsors identify periods of their modern history as effectively as any other marker. Real Madrid's partnership with Siemens from 2002 to 2006 covered the *Galácticos* era, where the club's policy of hoarding superstars brought glamour but not the tenth Champions League trophy, *La Décima*, that they craved. In contrast, the period with Emirates from 2013 to date marks the club picking up five Champions League titles in nine seasons, dominating the competition in a manner not seen since the five consecutive titles they won in the 1950s.

While sponsorship is often thought of as a modern invention, several US teams sported a brand's name over a century ago. St Louis sides Scullin Steel and Vesper Buick bore the name of their backers on the centre of their shirts during the US Open Cup finals in the early 1920s. The first appearance of company branding on European football shirts occurred during the Second World War. Clubs were eager to ensure that their stars were exempt from military service, and the strategically important automotive sector offered a route to exemption for employees. Therefore, the Turin clubs were rebranded as Fiat Turin and Cisitalia Juventus respectively, with the Fiat logo appearing on the teams' shirts in 1943/44. These pairings were unusual given Juventus's association with the Agnelli family, which founded Fiat in 1899 and has also run Juventus since 1923 with only a brief break in the 1940s.

Similar postwar arrangements made for economic reasons saw Lanerossi Vicenza sport the 'R' logo of their textile industry owners from 1953 to 1990, while fellow Italian clubs Sarom Ravenna (1954–1964), Ozo Mantova (1955–1960), SimmenthalMonza (1955–1964) and Zenit Modena (for the 1957/58 season) had similar arrangements with their backers. Torino revisited the idea of sponsorship in 1958, with a 'T' on the right side of the chest signifying the link with the Talmone confectionery brand. Unfortunately, the team were relegated to Serie B for the first time that season, and superstition meant that all markings were removed from the shirt until 1971.

The first reported use of a sponsor independent of club ownership was by Uruguayan side Club Atlético Peñarol in the early 1950s. Star player Obdulio Varela refused to wear the sponsored shirts, stating, 'The time for having a ring put on their nose is over for black boys. You pay me to play soccer. If you want a man to wear posters, hire Fosforito [a famed Uruguayan showman].' Austria Vienna were the first

European team to feature a shirt sponsor, the Schwechater brewery's logo appearing on the front of their kit back in 1966. The following year, the wonderfully named second-tier side Wormatia Worms became the first German team to feature a sponsor as the Caterpillar firm's 'CAT' brand graced their strip. In an early example of competition sponsorship, from 1968 all sides competing in the Coupe de France wore bottled water company Vittel's logo on their shirt. To this day, during matches in the competition the clubs sport the cup's sponsors rather than their own backer.

One of the most well-known examples of early football sponsorships is German liquor producer Jagermeister's appearance on Eintracht Braunschweig's jersey. This is largely thanks to an iconic photo of controversial German international Paul Breitner wearing the sponsored strip during his solitary season at the club in 1977/78. Having created a motor-racing team to promote their brand in 1972, the company's CEO Günter Mast was looking for other innovative forms of promotion. He attended a party with other prominent businessmen and was struck by how many disappeared to watch West Germany's European Championship quarter-final encounter with England. He realised that – in contrast to its working-class roots – football was a game enjoyed by the whole population offering fantastic marketing opportunities. Local team Braunschweig were in financial trouble and welcomed an agreement to have the firm sponsor their shirts. The DFB rejected the move, but Mast persuaded the club to change their badge from a red lion to the company's deer head logo. The new design debuted against

Schalke 04 in March 1973, and by the end of the year the DFB permitted overt shirt sponsorships.

In England, the case for shirt sponsorship was fought by ex-Northern Ireland international Derek Dougan, who combined his roles as player, manager and chief executive for non-league Kettering Town with being chairman of the Professional Footballers' Association. Having agreed a four-figure sum for shirt sponsorship with local tyre firm Kettering Tyres, the sponsor debuted in a Southern League match against Bath City in January 1976. The Football Association ordered him to remove it, but instead Dougan had new shirts made with 'KETTERING T' embroidered on them which he claimed stood for the club's name. Having deliberated for a couple of months, the FA sent a threat of a £1,000 fine which led Dougan to remove the sponsor. He continued to battle the FA and having enlisted clubs including Derby County and Bolton Wanderers to fight the ban, it was overturned for the start of the 1977/78 season although the sponsor logo size was limited.

Despite this victory, clubs faced a further obstacle as TV companies refused to show live matches or highlights involving teams with shirt sponsors. In the BBC's case, this was because it conflicted with restrictions on advertising within the licence agreement, whereas commercial station ITV saw shirt sponsorship as offering product placement without payment on their channel. Coventry City, under the chairmanship of *Match of the Day* pundit Jimmy Hill, channelled Derek Dougan's spirit in trying to circumvent the restrictions. Having signed a sponsorship deal with local car manufacturer Talbot, the club's request to change their name to Coventry Talbot was rejected. Undeterred, they incorporated the company's T logo into the design of their shirts but they were not permitted to wear them during televised games.

As a result of the restrictions, sponsor uptake was slow, compounded by concerns about tarnishing the integrity of clubs' kits. Hibernian were the first British side to sport a shirt sponsor in 1977/78, with long-established manufacturer Bukta adorning their new kit. Liverpool were early adopters in England, signing a £50,000 deal with Hitachi in 1979, while neighbours Everton sported Danish meat firm Hafnia the same year. Arsenal signed a £500,000 three-year deal with JVC in 1981, with Manchester United's Sharp sponsorship following in 1982 and Tottenham Hotspur's Holsten deal in 1983. The same year, a new TV deal was struck permitting live league fixtures and shirts bearing sponsors but at half the size permitted by the FA. Following this release of restrictions, the spread of shirt sponsorship was such that by 1987 all Football League clubs had a deal. However, the relative profile of the top clubs meant that shirt sponsorship was an early driver of growing financial inequity in the professional game, with combined shirt sponsorship of teams in the top four divisions in 1988 being £12.8m, £2.8m, £1.6m and £900,000 respectively.

In Italy, creative solutions were also sought to bypass sponsorship restrictions. While the Italian Football Federation banned shirt sponsorship, nothing was mentioned about shorts and so in 1978 Udinese owner Teofilio Sanson added his ice-cream firm's logo to his club's kit. The 10m lira fine was not enough to discourage Vicenza president Giuseppe Farina from employing a similar level of ingenuity the following season. Clubs were allowed to display a 12cm^2 manufacturer's logo on the shirt, so the Ponte pasta factory was rebranded as Ponte sportswear and included on the shirt in an August 1979 Coppa Italia game against Roma. Star player Paolo Rossi's shirt did not feature the logo due to a personal agreement he had with another food company, Polenghi Lombardo. This was ironic, as a key motivation for the sponsorship was to fund the player's purchase. A larger fine of 20m lira followed, and the sponsor was removed, but on 23 March 1980 the logo reappeared and was sported by all 11 players including Rossi. The IFF relented and authorised shirt sponsors from the start of the 1981/82 season. This included Inter Milan, whose shirts sported the Inno-Hit brand only a couple of years after club president Ivanoe Fraizzoli said that sponsors would appear 'over my dead body'.

The Spanish league was relatively late in adopting shirt sponsors, Real Madrid's Zanussi tie-up being the first high-profile deal in 1982. A few leading clubs refused to feature sponsors for much longer, Athletic Club of Bilbao finally adding local oil and gas company Petronor in 2008. Similarly, Barcelona did not capitalise on their worldwide profile until 2006, thereafter paying charity UNICEF to feature their logo from 2006 to 2011 (although Catalan public broadcaster TV3 had featured as a sleeve sponsor since 2004). They completed a controversial about-face in 2011, agreeing a five-year £150m deal with the Qatar Foundation. The league has also seen one of the longest-term deals, with French carmaker Citroën featuring on Celta Vigo's shirts from 1986 to 2016.

Some clubs that began as works teams still retain a strong link to the company. As with the early examples of Fiat Turin and Vesper Buick, for several clubs in the modern era the founding organisation has served as their primary sponsor. The city of Wolfsburg was founded in 1938 to house workers for Volkswagen's Beetle factory, and in 1945 VfL Wolfsburg – now of the Bundesliga – was established as a club for the company's employees. The Volkswagen brand has served as VfL's front-of-shirt sponsor since the 1980s. Similar situations saw PSV Eindhoven sponsored by electronics giant Philips until 2016, and Leverkusen's shirts featuring the name of pharmaceutical company Bayer and their brands including Aspirin and Alka-Seltzer until 2000. Although not founded by the company, the stable of clubs purchased by Red Bull including RB Leipzig, Red Bull Salzburg and New York Red Bulls feature the energy drink brand's trademark. Controversy has recently arisen in this area over the clubs taken over by organisations closely linked to nation states, such as Manchester City, Paris Saint-Germain and Newcastle United. In several cases, front-of-shirt sponsorships have been agreed with companies from the same state for a high fee, with both media sources and governing bodies raising concerns that these deals may be artificially inflated to circumvent financial regulations.

While many shirt sponsors are plonked unceremoniously on to the shirt, some designs have used novel approaches to promoting products. Between 2003 and 2005, Atlético Madrid were sponsored by Colombia Pictures who used the space to promote newly released movies including *Spiderman*, *Hellboy* and *Hitch*. Similarly, Barcelona's 2022 sponsorship deal with music-streaming platform Spotify saw different artists showcased on the team's shirt. The owl logo of Canadian rapper Drake's OVO record label was the first to feature for the *El Clásico* game against Real Madrid in October, celebrating his 50 billionth stream on the platform.

Rather than change within a brand, English side Notts County signed different deals with ten sponsors including Nottingham-born musician and Magpies fan Jake Bugg, so that each appeared on the shirt for one month of the 2017/18 season. Fans wanting to buy replica shirts were given the choice to have a sponsorless version or one with any of the ten brands printed on the front. For 2020/21 new main sponsor Cadbury donated their home shirt sponsorship to local travel firm Sharpes of Nottingham, one of many local firms impacted by the Covid-19 pandemic. Again, the scheme was seen as successful and has since been repeated for the following two seasons with Access Training replacing Sharpes in 2022/23. In a similar vein, since 2011, Liverpool sponsor Standard Chartered have donated their front-of-shirt spot to a charitable initiative linked to the brand for one game per season. Most recently, for the Premier League match against Manchester City in October 2022, the team sported the Futuremakers initiative aimed at reducing inequalities through education and training.

Barcelona had previously innovated with sponsor placement in 2013 as part of a £15m, five-year deal with Intel. They put the

Intel Inside logo upside down on the inside of the shirt so that it could only be revealed by lifting the shirt up to display the 'Inside'. In a similar vein, Getafe printed a Burger 'King' on the inside of their shirts in addition to the logo on the front, so that players celebrating by lifting their shirt could appear to be wearing a promotional mask. For the opening game of the 2018 season, Brazilian team Corinthians partnered with Unilever to promote their anti-odour soap OMO. The sponsor panel appeared white, only appearing as the wearer's sweat was absorbed by the fabric, although in some cases it failed to emerge. Breaking the usual trend of horizontal sponsors, a huge Paddy Power logo was printed diagonally across Huddersfield Town's shirt in a friendly in 2019. The stunt aimed to highlight the betting company's 'Save Our Shirts' campaign, urging fellow businesses to remove shirt sponsors. For breaking sponsorship regulations, the club were fined £50,000 by the FA, although the global coverage the move attracted was certainly more valuable. With Huddersfield, and later Motherwell and Newport County, Paddy Power paid to sponsor the team but left the shirts sponsorless.

An increasing focus has been placed on the nature of the industries sponsoring football clubs, with betting companies attracting particular attention. The first UK gambling sponsorship was Fulham's 2002 deal with Betfair, and soon the growing internet betting market drew new companies. This was fuelled by changes in legislation such as the UK 2005 Gambling Act, as whereas only bingo and lottery products could be advertised on TV and radio this was now extended to all gambling products. By 2016/17, 50 per cent of the Premier

League teams had a betting firm on their shirts, attracted as much by the exposure in lucrative South Asian markets as by revenue in the UK. The potential for harm, particularly to children and adolescents, caused by promotion of these companies has been a constant topic of discussion. This was highlighted in 2009 when it was revealed that SBObet and 188bet, who sponsored multiple Premier League team shirts, were offering live betting markets on Premier League academy football and youth international competitions. Growing concern about gambling firm advertising has led to several major competitions restricting their inclusion on football shirts. In 2018 and 2020, Italy and Spain respectively banned new gambling sponsors with ongoing deals allowed to run until 2019 and 2022 while a planned ban in the UK has been delayed.

Alcohol sponsorship was widespread in the UK in the early stages of the sponsorship era, beginning with Newcastle United's 20-year partnership with Scottish & Newcastle Brewery from 1980. Four leading sides featured alcohol sponsors in the inaugural Premier League season of 1992/93, but the rise of gambling sponsors meant that no side in the competition has had an alcohol sponsor since 2017. Alcohol sponsorship was banned in France in 1991, while sponsorship by alcohol above 20 per cent ABV was banned in Spain in 2012. As with gambling, there is particular concern about the potential effects on children, with the UK drinks industry voluntarily removing alcohol sponsors from children's kits in 2007.

Most recently, cryptocurrency firms have begun to appear on several leading clubs' shirts as sponsors. While this industry is still in its infancy, already it has been criticised for multiple reasons including the lack of stability, potential for fraud and use in money laundering and even the environmental cost of energy used to mine the currencies. Wolverhampton Wanderers were the first Premier League team to feature a company from this industry on their jersey. In 2018/19, the logo of cryptocurrency exchange CoinDeal (whose founder was charged with fraud in January 2023) appeared on the West Midlands side's sleeve. Since then, Crystal Palace, Newcastle, Watford, Leicester City, Chelsea and Southampton have all adopted crypto sponsors with the latter two being the first to feature a firm as a primary shirt sponsor. Similarly, leading clubs Atlético Madrid and Sevilla in Spain, Borussia Mönchengladbach in Germany and Roma, Atalanta, Inter Milan and Lazio in Italy are among those with a crypto backer on the front of their shirt in the 2022/23 season. The volatility of this industry was demonstrated only a month into the season, when Inter Milan looked to replace primary sponsor Digitalbits after the company began missing scheduled payments.

Football finance expert Kieran Maguire explains the motivations of clubs who make agreements with these firms, 'I use the phrased blinded by the cheque. Sponsors come along from the gambling or crypto industries who are prepared to pay more than other industries. Recently, I spoke to the commercial director of a former Premier League club, who told me that if they go to a gambling company they could secure sponsorship revenue of £7m per season. If they approached a company in finance or transport they would likely be offered around £2m annually. Regardless of the moral/ethical side, that £5m pays for two extra players' wages. It's not illegal and clubs are prepared to take that risk for a high reward.' He also spoke about the motivations of the sponsors, 'To date over 1,000 crypto currencies have gone bust. It's an unregulated, highly volatile, easily manipulated product that is still in the embryonic stage of development. These companies want legitimacy and normalisation of their industry, and one way of doing this is partnering with an established club.'

Beer, gambling and crypto sponsors appear quite tame compared to some of the firms drafted in to support cash-hungry clubs. Greek side Paleopyrgo sported a local funeral parlour on their strips, completing the look by playing in black shirts with white crosses on the front. Less sombrely, Austrian side Wiener Viktoria, managed by national team legend Toni Polster, featured the brand of cannabis growers Flowery Fields as front-of-shirt sponsor in 2017. Scarborough FC were sponsored by Black Death Vodka in 1990/91 although the shirt was later banned by the FA, while adult-themed comic *Viz* featured on Blyth Spartans' kit in 1993. Greek side Voukefalas featured local brothel Soula on their strips in 2012, while in 2017, US amateur side Washington Square FC of Brookline, Massachusetts emblazoned adult website RedTube on their kit. Similarly, German sixth-division side SV Oberwürzbach displayed adult film star Lena Nitro's website, before the regional FA banned the deal on ethical grounds. Less explicably, the DFB banned FC Homburg's deal with condom manufacturers London in the

1987/88 season, with the logo appearing the following season after the side took the federation to court.

The nature of sponsors' business or the company's behaviour has also led to deals being cancelled following fan or media pressure. Atlético Madrid's deal with the Azerbaijan tourist board between 2012 and 2015 was stopped after human rights organisations protested about the country's record. More recently, German side Schalke cancelled their 15-year association with their Russian state-owned shirt sponsor Gazprom after the country's invasion of Ukraine. Newly promoted Premier League side Norwich City tore up their contract with Asian gambling firm BK8 after the latter were found to have promoted their platform using highly sexualised images of women, sparking outrage from fans.

While one of the aims of companies investing in football sponsorship is to promote the brand among the club's fans, it could also alienate supporters of opposing teams. To that end, bitter Glaswegian rivals Celtic and Rangers have been sponsored by the same brand in periods with CR Smith (1984–1987), NTL (1999–2003), Carling (2003–2010) and Tennent's (2010–2013) to avoid a partial boycott by half of the divided city. Similarly, Buenos Aires sides River Plate and Boca Juniors both sported domestic beer brand Quilmes from 1995 to 2002.

The growth of women's football has led to opportunities to attract sponsorship from brands aiming to sell specifically to women, but this can also present challenges. Many of Europe's biggest clubs have developed a women's side as a 'sub-brand' of the men's team, with only a few high-profile examples such as Turbine Potsdam and Sweden's Umeå having a primarily female focus. 'I think that's really problematic for the future of the Women's Super League. Why would you want to see a Manchester United 'Lite'?' asked Professor Jean Williams. 'We describe the impulse to "shrink and pink" as a way to present women's football as a secondary product.' Not only does this limit their ability to develop a distinct identity and uniform but it may discourage potential sponsors who would otherwise welcome an opportunity to appeal to female football fans. Professor Williams said, 'I think the most problematic example of that is what's happening at Manchester City. The values of the City Group are not necessarily ones that are about female empowerment.' Given this, it is easy to understand why female-focused brands would not wish to support Saudi-backed Newcastle United or one of the UAE-funded clubs given restrictions on women's rights in these countries. Similarly, the high-profile cases involving violence against women perpetrated by footballers are unlikely to attract these companies to clubs with a primarily 'male' brand. Alternatives do exist, as Professor Williams identifies, 'A counter example is what's happening at Angel City [in Los Angeles]. It's not a sub-brand of a men's club and it's avowedly feminist in its values, being owned by a largely female group of media and sports stars.'

For many of the clubs in the English Premier League, such as Arsenal, Manchester United and Chelsea, both men's and women's teams feature the same sponsor. Other leading European women's sides feature a backer that is distinct from the men's team. For example, Barcelona Femení sport the brand of the world's largest tool company, Stanley Black and Decker, on their strip with the men's side sponsored by Spotify. Interestingly, Ajax Vrouwen feature the classic vertical ABN-AMRO brand which supported the men's side from 1992 to 2009. Having won five KNVB Women's Cups and two top-tier Women's Eredivisie titles in only ten years of existence, we may yet see the team/sponsor combo at the peak of European football as when the men's team captured the Champions League trophy in 1995.

The financial explosion of the football industry over the past three decades can be charted in the changing profile of the sponsors worn by leading clubs. A snapshot of the first Premier League kit sponsors shows seven electronics firms including three firms based in the growing home-computer industry. Aside from the four alcohol sponsors, two sporting goods firms, two pharmaceutical companies, an automotive firm, a building society, a radio station, a timber merchant and a tool retailer complete the varied line-up, with Sheffield Wednesday and Wimbledon lining up without a sponsor. In this era local sponsors were still evident with Southampton's Draper Tools, Fisons from Ipswich, Norwich and Peterborough Building Society and Sheffield's Laver timber yard fitting this category.

By 2022/23 the profile had changed such that eight gambling firms, five financial services firms, two airlines, two online car retailers and two telecommunications-related firms completed the list. Sponsorship of the 'big six' Premier League teams is now the sole preserve of massive multinationals, with the median annual turnover of their sponsors over $10bn. The increasing value of sponsorship deals over time can be illustrated directly by the example of Manchester United. Their first sponsor, Sharp, paid just £100,000 per year over a five-year deal in 1982, but by 2000 new sponsor Vodafone's four-year deal was worth £7.5m annually. The value continued to increase with new deals with Aon (2009, £20m per year), and Chevrolet (2014, £53m per year) although United's performance on the field likely contributed to a slight drop to £47m annually for 2021's TeamViewer deal. This dwarfs fellow Premier League clubs Burnley and Brighton & Hove Albion's deals in the same year, which were only £1.5m per season.

In several cases, wealthy fans have stepped in to sponsor their favourite team with musicians particularly keen on the practice. Scottish band Wet Wet Wet backed their local club Clydebank FC from 1993 to 1997 with their name appearing on shirts, while Welsh band Super Furry Animals appeared on Cardiff City's tops during their Welsh Cup run in 1999. Compatriots Goldie Lookin' Chain sponsored hometown team Newport County in 2004/05, although a GLC-inspired strip was removed from sale in 2021 after Burberry threatened legal action due to the use of the brand's distinctive pattern. Ipswich Town fan and musician Ed Sheeran has also paid for his Mathematics tour logo to appear on his team's strip from 2021 to 2023. Having made his footballing debut while on a season's loan to the club, England footballer Harry Kane has sponsored Leyton Orient since 2020, donating the space to support charities.

Most shirt sponsors appear horizontally, with a few notable exceptions. Ajax placed local bank ABN-AMRO's logo vertically on their 1990s shirts, allowing it to merge seamlessly with their central red stripe in a style which has been retained by the women's team through their ongoing deal with the financial giant. Juventus featured a diagonal Sony and Minidisc sponsor on their change goalkeeper and unworn third kit in 1996, while Borussia Dortmund backer Evonik's logo was incorporated into a diagonal sash design for the 2008/09 away kit. For Inter Milan's centenary shirt, the design team wrestled with where best to put the sponsor on the St George's cross which filled the shirt. Club owner Massimo Moratti solved the issue, telling them to shrink the patch and put it unobtrusively under the club's crest.

While sides initially operated with a single primary sponsor on the front of the shirt, in many competitions outside of the large European leagues, multiple sponsors are permitted, with clubs taking full advantage of this freedom. In 2019, newly promoted French second division side FC Chambly Oise featured no fewer than nine commercial sponsors on their shirt with two further logos promoting their region. The club defended their approach, highlighting that their relatively low profile and low population (10,000) of their town did not allow them to attract a wealthy primary sponsor. Even in the most high-profile leagues, separate sleeve sponsors have commonly been adopted to boost commercial revenue. In 2017/18 the Premier League allowed sleeve sponsors which provide a smaller but substantial boost to sponsor revenue (typically ten to 25 per cent of the main sponsor value). For example, Manchester United's £47m-per-year TeamViewer deal is around five times higher than their sleeve deal with Kohler, worth £10m each season. In 2006/07, Football League clubs were allowed to feature a secondary sponsor on the reverse of the shirt, an option not taken up by the Premier League.

In 1982, UEFA permitted shirt sponsors and manufacturer logos for most of the competition with the sponsors being removed for the finals. Sponsor provisions were further restricted with the advent of the Champions League in 1992. Having agreed exclusive deals with eight competition sponsors who also had a monopoly on pitchside advertising boards, UEFA banned all shirt sponsors from the competition for the first two seasons. When sponsors were permitted, they were restricted in size and complexity such that Opel-sponsored teams removed the manufacturer's 'lightning' logo and Borussia Dortmund were left with only the 'C' logo of their sponsor Die Continentale. Restrictions on the use of manufacturer logos in designs meant that Barcelona wore a cup shirt without Kappa logo taping on its sleeves, while Kelme's paw print logo was removed from Real Madrid's shirt sleeves as they clinched the continental title in 1998. Similarly, Ajax, winners of the first Champions League Final to feature sponsors in 1995, wore an adapted home shirt design without Umbro sleeve taping earlier in the competition.

Relatively few examples of international shirt sponsors exist due to regulations against their use in competitive matches, which cynics would suggest helps governing bodies such as UEFA and FIFA increase central sponsor revenue. In addition, many countries' football teams are under the auspices of the government sports ministry making overt commercial deals problematic. One notable exception is replica Republic of Ireland jerseys, which since 1986 have included Opel, Eircom and then 3 as traditional sponsors despite an inability for player shirts to sport their backer's logo. While removed from the sporting action on the pitch, they still offer nostalgia to ROI fans due to the number being worn during major tournaments. The Brazilian Football Confederation subtly sneaked the logo of coffee firm Café do Brasil on to their crest in the early 1980s (including for World Cup matches), an approach also taken by the Ivory Coast team with Café de Côte d'Ivoire. The South American side featured Coca-Cola's logo on their shirts in a 1987 friendly as part of the firm's sponsorship of the national league. Finally, Sweden and Finland routinely sported sponsors during friendlies in the 1980s, while several sides including Iceland, Thailand, Colombia and Australia have also featured brand logos on their strips.

The Printing

'IT'S NOT about the name of the back of the jersey, it's about the badge on the front.' This quote from former England captain David Beckham has been challenged in recent years with the rise of international footballing megastars like Cristiano Ronaldo whose personal wealth, social media reach and commercial value is greater than that of many leading clubs and national sides. A player's individual image rights now form a key part of their contract with a club, and many have a dedicated 'brand' allowing them to exploit their sporting fame for commercial gain.

Similarly, tensions have developed between individual member clubs and organisations like UEFA over the distribution and security of competition revenue leading to the looming spectre of a breakaway European Super League. These modern commercial battles are also played out on the real estate of modern shirts. Manufacturer, sponsor, clubs and nation branding competes with player names and numbers for space on cluttered jerseys, whose appearance can vary dramatically for the same side depending on the regulations of each competition. This is a very different picture from the first century of football, when there were very few details on a shirt that would identify an individual team or player other than their colour.

The earliest element of personalisation to feature on football shirts was the team badge, first worn in the England v Scotland international in 1872. England wore the three lions used by King Richard I in his Great Seal in 1198, whereas their opponents took the lion rampant from the Royal Banner of Scotland. As discussed in 'The Colour', in the early decades of football history shirts served a primarily practical purpose and club identities were fairly fluid. Clubs were seen as representatives of their region at national-level cup and league competition, and would commonly sport regional coats of arms rather than a club-specific design. The first example is Aston Villa displaying Birmingham's city crest in their 1887 FA Cup Final win against West Bromwich Albion. The expense of reproducing complex coats of arms meant that club sides would only use them for important matches. For regular league and cup games, monograms or simple shapes, such as a Maltese cross or star, would be worn.

The percentage of Football League clubs who wore their badge on their home shirt remained low until the 1930s, thereafter climbing steadily from ten per cent until all clubs had adopted a badge by the mid-1990s. Bayern Munich (1989), Juventus (1994) and AC Milan (1995) are among the elite teams who were late to adopt a crest on their regular shirts. Generally, crests were more readily adopted at international level with only five South American teams in the inaugural 13-team World Cup in 1930 omitting a badge from their shirt. By the 1970 edition of the tournament, all teams included their emblem on their playing kit.

Many clubs continued to use regional symbols rather than their own designs until the 1970s, Manchester United wearing the city coat of arms in their 1968 European Cup Final win against Benfica. In the 1970s, English league clubs such as Leeds United, Everton and Crystal Palace featured the team's name or initials rather than a crest. Real Madrid were pioneers in this area, as the interlocking MCF monogram from their inaugural crest (prior to their royal designation) survives to this day. This trend prefaced the explosion in use of copyrighted crests in the 1970s as part of the replica shirt boom. For many international teams, a national animal or their flag or national crest is the inspiration, and, similarly, clubs focus on local landmarks or symbols. Liverpool's badge features the mythical liver bird, whereas city rivals Everton's crest is dominated by the local 18th-century St Rupert's Tower – a lock-up for drunks and petty criminals. The bearded, pipe-smoking sailor silhouette on Sampdoria's badge is Genoa's patron saint Baciccia (John the Baptist), whereas Roma's shield features city folklore founders Romulus and Remus with their mother wolf. For the club's 2022/23 third shirt, manufacturer New Balance used holographic technology to create two versions of the crest. At certain angles the regular crest would appear, but on tilting the shirt the image changed to a stylised monogram logo used in the early 1930s. Unsurprisingly, this did not meet with UEFA regulations and the shirt featured a standard crest on its debut appearance in a Europa League tie against HJK Helsinki. Club-specific icons are also represented with FC Köln's crest featuring Hennes the goat, originally gifted to the club by a travelling circus. Less romantically, energy drink company Red Bull's logo features prominently in the crests of its stable of clubs including Leipzig, Salzburg and New York. Adidas left their own subtle imprint on Manchester United's crest when manufacturing the team's kits during the 1980s. The German brand added football boots in place of scrolls in the top corners of the design, with each boot bearing the three stripes synonymous with the company.

In recent years many clubs have moved to simplify their crest to provide a more marketable logo across social media and ventures outside football. In 2017 Juventus replaced a logo introduced in 2004 containing a bull, crown, black and white stripes and the club name with two stripes creating a 'J'. There was uproar from fans, accusing the board of erasing a core piece of the club's history. While it is understandable that these symbols are close to supporters' hearts, the response ignores the almost continual evolution of crests over their history. For example, from 1979 to 1990 the Juventus emblem was a simple zebra silhouette before a more complex design was adopted. Similarly, Liverpool replaced a complex crest with a liver bird logo and their initials in 2012. This is much more faithful to the simple designs used in the club's heyday from 1950 until the late 1980s. In contrast to these dramatic evolutions, Barcelona's crest has remained largely unaltered since 1910. Martyn Routledge and Elspeth Wills's excellent book *The Beautiful Badge: The Stories Behind the Football Club Badge* covers the origins and development of club badges for those wanting the complete history.

Although the numbers 1-11 are entrenched in football culture, numbered shirts only emerged in Europe in the 1920s. Australian and New Zealand sides were the first recorded teams to use shirt numbers around 1904, the idea transferring from rugby and allowing spectators to identify individual players. The number systems were not uniform; some excluded the goalkeeper and, in contrast to modern conventions, numbering typically began with the forwards. The first official recognition is given to the 1911 match between Sydney Leichardt and HMS Powerful, according to the International Federation of Football History and Statistics's official website. In the same year, player numbers were mandated for competitive matches in New South Wales. In England, numbered shirts first appeared in an amateur game between Wanderers and Corinthians on 23 March 1914. Later, Scullin Steel of the American Soccer League wore numbers on the reverse of their shirts in the 1923 Challenge Cup Final. This is not the only example from the US, with film footage from the US Open Cup Final on 30 March 1924 showing Vesper Buick wearing numbered shirts against the Fall River Marksmen.

While South America was slower to adopt some shirt innovations, photographs from Third Lanark's summer 1923 tour show both the Scottish club and representative side Zona Norte wearing numbers on the front of their shirts. Shirt numbers were first used by professional teams in England when Arsenal and Chelsea wore them unofficially during the opening two games of the 1928/29 Football League season. The first sanctioned use of numbers was in the 1933 FA Cup Final, where

Everton wore 1-11 and their opponents Manchester City 12-22. They were adopted by England in a trial match against potential England players ('The Rest') on 22 March 1933. Thereafter, it was another four years until they wore them in a friendly against Norway on 14 May 1937. The Football League Committee rejected proposals to require shirt numbers in its 1933 and 1934 annual general meetings, accepting arguments that it would cost too much and tarnish the purity of clubs' colours. Their use was finally made mandatory in the 1939/40 season, helping both referees and fans to identify players.

While numbered shirts appeared in Scotland in the 1940s, they were not made compulsory until 1960. Celtic refused to comply, chairman Bob Kelly claiming it would sully the club's famous green and white hoops, while director Desmond White protested that their shirt design 'did not lend itself to numbers'. This latter view was supported when the team donned numbered shirts for a friendly against Sedan in 1960, with the yellow numbers clashing with the kit and proving difficult to read. The club adopted numbered shorts instead, using shirt numbers in a competitive match for the first time in a European Cup Winners' Cup tie against Boavista in 1975 after UEFA mandated their use. Interestingly, while numbers 12-16 were assigned to substitutes, clubs were allowed to omit the number 13 on the basis of superstition. In domestic games, Celtic held out until 1994/95 when the Scottish Football League introduced a new rule mandating shirt numbering. Even then they wore numbers on their sleeves for the first two matches before finally donning traditionally numbered shirts for the Old Firm game at Ibrox.

Shirt numbers did not emerge at international level until 1937, when England's outfield players wore them against Scotland at Hampden Park. The following year they would appear for the first time in international competition at the World Cup in the modern 1-11 format for each team, although they were not adopted by everyone in the finals. Allocated squad numbers were first introduced for the World Cup in 1954, with teams largely conforming to a 1-11 format familiar to modern-day fans. The exception was Austria, who allocated by position such that their goalkeepers wore numbers 1-3. This was a scheme later adopted by other teams including the Soviet Union, Switzerland, Spain and Colombia in 1962. With the exception of goalkeepers (given 1, 21 and 22), in 1966 France assigned numbers alphabetically by surname in an effort to avoid conflicts over popular numbers. Argentina employed a similar system from 1974 to 1982, although from 1978 their goalkeepers were not exempt and numbered 3, 5 and 13 and 2, 7 and 16 in the two competitions. Perhaps unsurprisingly, star player Diego Maradona (originally 12) was allowed to swap with Patricio Hernández in order to wear his usual 10 in 1982. The Netherlands also numbered their players (including goalkeepers) in the same way in 1974, with the exception that Johan Cruyff retained his number 14 shirt despite being the first player in alphabetical order. The naming system was later briefly revived by Argentina coach Daniel Passarella for the 1997 Copa América, with goalkeeper Nacho González taking 10. While England adopt the mandated squad numbers at major finals, they use numbers 1-11 for starters in all other international fixtures.

The North American Soccer League was the first club competition to include designated squad numbers, featuring from the 1971 season. The first European club match to feature squad numbers saw Arsenal beat Sheffield Wednesday in the 1993 League Cup Final, the Gunners repeating the feat the following month in the FA Cup Final against the same opponents when squad numbers were also worn. From August of the same year they were introduced to the Premier League. Charlton Athletic were one of only ten Football League teams to adopt permanent squad numbers at the same time, employing an alphabetical approach such that Scottish defender Stuart Balmer wore 1. They abandoned the system the following year, while fellow Football League side Brighton & Hove Albion and Premier League Arsenal ditched them midway through 1993/94, the Gunners reverting to squad numbers from 1994/95 onwards. A year before this, the 1992 European Championship saw the first appearance of player names on shirts at international tournaments. Charlton Athletic were also the last Premier League club for over 20 years to line up in a match with the traditional numbers 1-11, following their promotion from the Football League in 1998 where assigned numbers were not used. Burnley finally repeated the feat in 2021 in a match against Liverpool at Anfield.

Permanent squad numbers were also introduced in Italy's Serie A and B, and to Spain's La Liga, in 1995. Spanish clubs were only allowed to assign numbers 1-25, with goalkeepers given 1, 13 and 25 and youth players using numbers 26 to 50. As recounted by midfielder Francesco Flachi to the Jersey Vice website, at the beginning of the season the Fiorentina players organised an auction to assign the new numbers with the proceeds donated to charity. The bidding began at 500,000 lira (about £25) for less desirable shirt numbers whereas those of the star players like Francesco Toldo, Gabriel Batistuta and Rui Costa began at 2.5m lira. With the Portuguese playmaker having talked constantly about wanting to secure his usual number 10 shirts, his team-mates colluded to push the price up to 5m lira. While squad numbers are commonly used in the Dutch league, they are not compulsory, and following relegation from the Eredivisie in 2010 Sparta Rotterdam adopted numbers 1-11 in games as a nod to tradition. In another example of strict Coupe de France regulations, players are only allowed to wear numbers 1-20 with the starting team wearing 1-11.

While formations have changed, the designation of some shirt numbers for particular positions is well established. Number 1 is for a goalkeeper, whereas the goal poacher dons 9 and the creative hub of a team is assigned 10. Johan Cruyff was the first high-profile footballer to regularly wear a number outside the usual starting choices, adopting his now-iconic 14 in club football in the 1970s. Having been injured, he returned for a match against PSV Eindhoven on 30 October. Midfielder Gerrie Mühren's usual number 6 shirt had been mislaid by the kit man and Cruyff offered his 9 and took 14 instead. They won, and at Cruyff's suggestion they retained their new numbers. Cruyff would also wear the same shirt in European matches including the 1971 European Cup Final, where unused substitute Ruud Suurendonk donned 5.

The introduction of club squad numbers allowed players to become more creative with their choices with some more justifiable than others. Ajax starlet Abdelhak Nouri collapsed during a friendly match after suffering a cardiac arrhythmia aged 20, and the resultant brain damage forced him to retire from football. While the club retired his number 34 shirt, touchingly many of his former team-mates including Donny van de Beek (Manchester United), Justin Kluivert (Roma) and Sofyan Amrabat (Fiorentina) adopted his number at their new clubs in tribute. Gianluigi Donnarumma wore number 99 for AC Milan to denote his year of birth, with the same reason given for the club's 2008 signings Ronaldinho, Mathieu Flamini and Andriy Shevchenko registering as 80, 84 and 76 respectively. Bixente Lizarazu's choice of 69 for a second spell at Bayern Munich was based on his birth year, but also height (1.69m) and weight (69kg). Mesut Özil's 67 at Fenerbahçe referenced his hometown's postcode, whereas David Beckham took the number 23 shirt at Real Madrid in tribute to basketball legend Michael Jordan. While many youth players make their first appearance in a high-numbered shirt and obtain lower numbers when more established, Liverpool's Trent Alexander-Arnold (66) and Chelsea's John Terry (26) are among those to retain their original assignments.

Due to the popularity of certain shirts, players have had to resort to mathematical means to emulate their preferred choice. Inter Milan striker Iván Zamorano famously wore '1+8' on his strip, having chosen to give up his number 9 shirt for Brazilian legend Ronaldo. Italy striker Mario Balotelli has worn 45 for the same reason throughout his career, while Derek Riordan chose 01 following his return to Hibernian as the number 10 was taken. Winger Denílson claimed that he was assigned the number 20 shirt for Brazil because 'I'm twice as good as the number 10', although this was not supported by his form after a world-record move from São Paulo to Real Betis in 1998.

Among squad number choices most likely to enrage traditionalists are those adopting numbers 1-11 in conflict with their primary position. Forwards Clint Dempsey, Wilfried Bony (both 2) and Asamoah Gyan (3) adopted numbers typically associated with defenders. In contrast, defenders Khalid Boulahrouz of Chelsea (9), William Gallas of Arsenal and Chievo goalkeeper Cristiano Lupatelli (both 10) all took spots typically reserved for forwards. While whole numbers are the accepted format, HJK Helsinki midfielder Mika Lehkosuo's sponsor deal with a local radio station saw him briefly don 96.2 on the reverse of his shirt before UEFA stepped in. Due to an oddity in Asian Cup player registration regulations, Australian winger Tommy Oar debuted against Indonesia wearing the number 121 shirt. In a similar vein, as all Mexican Liga MX youth players must be assigned a squad number, Edson Álvarez retained his number 282 shirt when appearing for his side Club América.

The importance of popular squad numbers combined with the growth of individual footballers' brands means that their assignment can lead to issues with player morale. Manchester United's French striker Anthony Martial was assigned 9 as his squad number following his initial £36m move from Monaco in 2015. Together with his management team, he developed an AM9 brand including a website, in the style of former Manchester United player Cristiano Ronaldo's CR7 moniker. However, the following year United signed 34-year-old Swedish icon Zlatan Ibrahimović and assigned him Martial's squad number without notifying the Frenchman, who was given 11. Martial showed his displeasure in the most devastating way available to players in the social media era, by unfollowing the club's Twitter and Instagram accounts. Having scored 18 goals and recorded 11 assists in an impressive debut season while wearing his favoured number, Martial became a bit-part player for long periods under new boss José Mourinho. First Zlatan and then new signing Romelu Lukaku were the first-choice centre forward, the Belgian taking over the Swede's squad number. In 2019, Martial was reinstalled as number 9 by Mourinho's successor Ole Gunnar Solskjær and responded with 23 goals and 12 assists in 48 appearances, helping the team to a third-placed Premier League finish and semi-final appearances in the three domestic and European cups.

The number 7 at Manchester United is one of a handful of club and national team shirts to have acquired a near-mythical status, given the many icons who have worn it over the club's history. Northern Ireland international George Best is the earliest of United's players to be associated with the shirt, although he also commonly wore 11. The link with 7 was assured when he wore it during United's maiden European Cup triumph in 1968, scoring the first goal in extra time after the meeting with

Benfica had finished 1-1 after 90 minutes. Bryan Robson wore 7 across more than a decade as the club's inspirational captain and driving force after joining from West Bromwich Albion in 1981. The mantle was then passed over to Eric Cantona in 1992, the £1.2m signing from Leeds being the first player to be permanently assigned the numeral after the introduction of squad numbers the following season. Having inspired United to their first title in 26 years, the mercurial Frenchman was a key part in establishing the aura around United's 7. David Beckham and Cristiano Ronaldo both then wore it with aplomb, playing key roles as their respective teams both won a Champions League title and multiple Premier Leagues.

Since Ronaldo's move to Real Madrid in 2009, the extraordinary pedigree of the number has unsurprisingly proved difficult to maintain. While the attitude of players like Antonio Valencia (who wore it from 2012 to 2014) and Edinson Cavani (2020–2022) has been applauded by fans, neither had the impact of previous holders of the jersey. In other cases, high-profile signings like Ángel Di María (2014/15) and Alexis Sánchez (2017–2019) disappointed with both their attitudes and performances, and were quietly ushered out of the club. Even Ronaldo had mixed fortunes when returning to reclaim his old shirt in 2021. Having scored 24 goals in only 39 appearances amid a disappointing 2021/22 season for the team, disagreements over his role and playing time with new manager Erik ten Hag led to the former Ballon d'Or winner leaving in mid-season amid a series of media outbursts which threatened to tarnish his Old Trafford legacy.

Another legendary figure which has proved a burden to its holders is the Argentinian number 10 shirt. Having led his national side to World Cup glory in Mexico in 1986 and to a loss in the 1990 final, Diego Maradona set a high bar by which future holders of the shirt would be judged. Talented players including Ariel Ortega, Pablo Aimar, Juan Román Riquelme and Carlos Tevez were all burdened with the task of replacing the football-mad country's greatest-ever player, with none truly succeeding at emulating the icon. Even Lionel Messi struggled with the demands of the role, his earlier disappointing senior international career contrasting with a list of individual and team honours won at club level. Having moved abroad at a young age, Messi was considered less of a true representative of the people than El Diego with his commitment to the national side being questioned despite leading his team to under-20 World Cup and Olympic titles in his youth. It was not until the tail end of his career, when he inspired his team to his first Copa América title in 2021 and World Cup glory in 2022 as the tournament's best player in each case, that he was considered to have proved himself a worthy successor to the country's most famous number 10. No doubt the search for the 'new Messi' will now begin, with each new pretender to the throne now aiming to exorcise two footballing ghosts.

A similar mystique surrounds the number 10 shirt of Argentina's fierce continental rivals Brazil, with Pelé, Zico, Rivaldo, Ronaldinho and Kaká previous custodians of the famous jersey now occupied by Neymar. In the women's game, fans wore US player Mia Hamm's number 9 shirt as she became the sport's first global superstar. Brazil striker Marta, often regarded as the greatest female footballer of all time, became another stellar name on the list of number 10s to play in her nation's yellow jersey. Outside of the traditional 11 numerals, veteran US player Megan Rapinoe has worn 15 for the majority of her international and club career including her decade (to date) with Seattle side OL Reign.

In a move adopted from American sports, several clubs have retired the squad numbers of particular players. Inter Milan's Javier Zanetti (4), West Ham's Bobby Moore, AC Milan's Franco Baresi (both 6) and Johan Cruyff (14) of Ajax are among those to have received this recognition of their long, successful careers. The honour has also been bestowed on behalf of players who passed away during their playing career, such as Davide Astori of Fiorentina and Cagliari (13), Espanyol's Daniel Jarque (21) and Manchester City's Marc-Vivien Foé (23). Dozens of clubs, including Bayern Munich, Lazio, Flamengo, Feyenoord, Sporting CP and Rangers have dedicated the number 12 to their fans ('the 12th man') and do not issue it to players.

When Juventus offered to retire Alessandro Del Piero's number 10 shirt after more than 700 appearances for the club, he refused, saying, 'I've really had so much that I would never want it to be retired, this way, every child can dream one day of wearing it.' Paolo Maldini's number 3 shirt for AC Milan was retired with the proviso that it could be reinstated if one of his children played for the club. While both of his sons played for the youth team, Christian was released without making an appearance. Younger son Daniel has become a bit-part player with the squad but plays in an attacking midfield role and hence he is unlikely to take up the sacred number.

As with numbers, the North American Soccer League was the first to introduce player naming on shirts in 1975. The Scottish national side experimented with player namesets in the late 1970s, beginning with a friendly against Peru in September 1979. The shirts featured players' names on the reverse in 13 home matches over the following two years before being discontinued. On one unfortunate occasion, Scotland wore shirt names on their new perforated Airtex away shirt for a British Home Championship match against Northern Ireland. The local sport shop Lumley's (now Greaves Sports) had used too low a temperature to apply the printing and the letters began to peel off mid-match, with players taking great delight in removing the misapplied letters from their team-mates' shirts.

Several teams experimented with player naming in the 1980s, such as AC Milan who wore named shirts in a 1980 Coppa Italia match. The following year, reigning European champions Nottingham Forest included player names on their strips in their International Cup loss against Uruguay's Nacional. The first major international tournament to feature player names was the 1992 European Championships, after which both this and World Cup tournaments retained the feature. As with many modern shirt developments, the Premier League was the first major European league to introduce shirt naming in 1993/94 with Serie A, the Bundesliga and La Liga following in 1995/96.

Due to their unwillingness to adopt squad numbers for international matches outside major tournaments, England did not feature player names in non-tournament games until 2001. Their first appearance was in a World Cup qualifier against Greece on 6 October where an injury-time David Beckham free kick sealed a 2-2 draw and qualification for the 2002 finals. In Germany, many teams feature the club's name (mandated in their regulations) above the number with the player name below to emphasise the importance of the club relative to the individual. In the early 1990s, a handful of German sides including Borussia Dortmund, Eintracht Frankfurt and St. Pauli also experimented with the orientation of their printing, featuring diagonal player numbers aligned with shirt patterns on the reverse. Although it did not feature on the pitch, this idea was taken one step further in 2018 when Andrés Iniesta announced that he was leaving Barcelona after more than 20 years. To celebrate his career, the club released a special-edition replica shirt with his number 8 rotated to display an infinity symbol.

Scotland's early Airtex error is not the only printing mishap to befall an unfortunate kit man, with several high-profile mistakes over the past 25 years. David Beckham winger was forced to line up with 'BECKAM' on his back for Manchester United's Charity Shield match against Chelsea in 1997. The English giants appear particularly prone to printing mishaps, with 'Andesron', John ,S'Hea', Tomasz 'Zuszczak' and Ole Gunnar 'Solksjaer' appearing on the club's shirts. Lucas 'Dgne' (France), David 'Betnley' (Tottenham), Zlatan 'Irbahimovic' (Juventus), Javier 'Mascerano' (Liverpool), Mauricio 'Wrigth' (Costa Rica) and Steven 'Gerrrad' (LA Galaxy) are among those to have sported a Pro Evolution Soccer-style nameset.

Sporting CP striker Liédson took the back-to-front 's' printed on his shirt as a lucky omen when he scored on his debut in 2002, wearing the same shirt for the remainder of a season that brought 19 goals in 36 appearances. It was unclear whether the supplier or kit man was at fault when the Brisbane Roar players' numbers began to peel off during an Asian Champions League qualifier against Ceres-Negros, the team being forced to apply sticky tape as a temporary fix. Republic of Ireland defender Richard Dunne had 5 drawn on to his back at pitchside by a coach during a European Championship qualifying game against Russia in 2011, after a blood injury exposed a lack of printed replacement shirts.

Not all errors are unintentional; when Sporting CP's players took to the field in March 2016 with misspelled names such as 'J Dario' (João Mário) and 'Guterres' (Teófilo Gutiérrez), it was part of a campaign from the club to persuade fans to avoid buying low-quality counterfeit merchandise. Similarly, England took to the field for the second half of their March 2022 friendly against Switzerland without names on their shirts in order to raise awareness about dementia.

These errors extend to other aspects of the shirt, with a cadre of eagle-eyed spotters always on hand to report even minor variations. During Rangers' Europa League play-off against Alashkert in 2021, winger Ryan Kent's shirt featured league sponsor 32Red instead of European sponsor Unibet sported by his team-mates, although luckily both companies were part of the same company. Aston Villa's Tyrone Mings took to the field for a Premier League match without an NHS 'Thank You' logo in June 2020, with the missing detail being applied at half-time. FC Union Berlin's kit man appeared to become confused by the club appearing in three competitions in their debut European season in 2022/23, as Portuguese centre-back Diogo Leite sported a DFB-Pokal sleeve patch during a Bundesliga game against RB Leipzig in August 2022. These mishaps have extended to wearing entirely the wrong kit, as in March 2011 when Spain substitute Fernando Llorente entered the pitch wearing a 2010 World Cup shirt rather than the current version. Similarly, in 2011 Italy's Mario Balotelli emerged for the second half of a friendly against Uruguay wearing a 2008 World Cup kit and had to change into his original shirt.

Number and namesets have evolved over time, becoming almost as varied and recognisable as the garments underneath them. This history is reported in detail in the beautiful and comprehensive *Football Type 2* by kit expert Denis Hurley and Manchester designer Rick Banks. Early numbers were sewn on, and therefore for ease of production and application they used simple, bold fonts until the 1970s. The growth of overt branding and team-specific designs in that decade saw a greater range of fonts and customisation. French sports manufacturer and retailer Somms produced the first branded numberset for the French national side in 1972, with the brand's logotype displayed on the bottom of each numeral. The 1974 World Cup saw the emergence of iconic styles including Adidas's three stripes worn by the likes of Poland, Zaire and Yugoslavia, and host West Germany's 3D shadow which would feature on top club and country strips for the following 25 years.

The South Team from the British Ladies' Football Club's inaugural match in 1895, which took place in front of a crowd of over 10,000 spectators. Even at this early stage, the recognisable silhouette of a female footballer's kit was emerging.

England line up against Scotland in 1955, wearing a lightweight, V-necked shirt. This 'Continental' style, made by Umbro, was inspired by the shirts worn by Hungary as they inflicted England's first defeat on home soil in November 1953.

Admiral's early 1980s England kits were some of the first to feature sublimated designs printed within the fabric, including this away shirt worn by Phil Thompson during the 1982 World Cup.

Manchester United's Diego Forlán had to be helped back into his Nike kit after celebrating a goal against Southampton in November 2002, as the dual-layer design made it difficult to put on when wet.

The advent of base layer garments around the turn of the millennium saw the popularity of traditional long-sleeved shirts decline.

Cameroon's sleeveless shirt worn at the 2002 Africa Cup of Nations (above). FIFA banned the shirt prior to that year's World Cup, forcing Puma to add loose sleeves which did not attach at the bottom in order to comply.

Palermo's pink and black colourway was adopted in 1907 (right), with club founder Count Giuseppe Airoldo proposing the 'sweet and sad' colours as a match for the team's inconsistent form. Credit: Richard Kelly

Bolivia's shirts at the 1930 World Cup in Uruguay spelled out a message for the competition hosts.

Sampdoria's iconic colourway, worn since their foundation via a merger in 1946, is one of the most distinctive in world football. Credit: Richard Kelly

Manchester United manager Sir Alex Ferguson ordered his players to change out of this grey third kit when 3-1 down against Premier League strugglers Southampton in April 1996. It was claimed that the shirt's colour prevented United's players from picking each other out against the crowd.

The shirts worn by West Germany and the Netherlands at the 1988 European Championship semi-final would go on to be two of the most sought-after for collectors.

The 1990s saw bolder designs appear, such as this Fiorentina 1991/92 away shirt by Italian manufacturer Lotto. All of the details, including the manufacturer and club logos and sponsor, are sublimated into the fabric. Credit: Richard Kelly

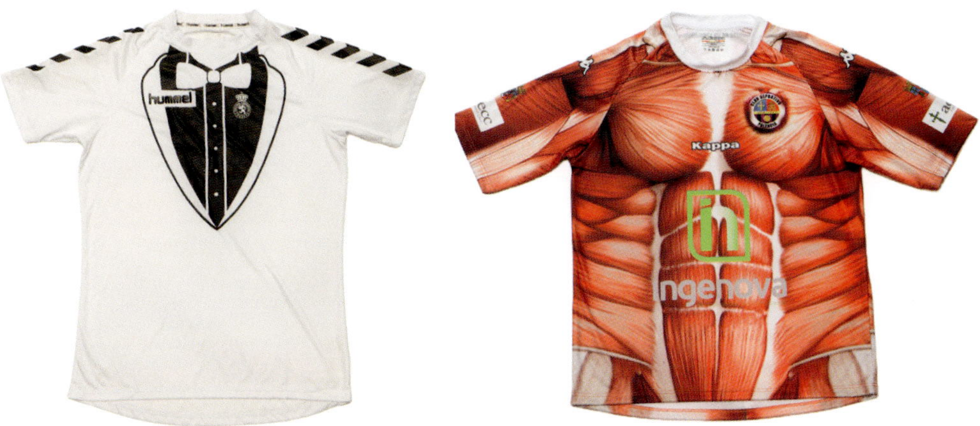

TV executive and ex-semi-professional player Juan Francisco Martin Fresneda spearheaded the development of a series of outrageous football kits for Spanish lower-division sides. This includes a white tuxedo design for Cultural's 90th anniversary in 2014/15 (left), and a muscle-themed strip for Palencia in 2015/16. Credit: Richard Kelly

US third-tier side Forward Madison's 'Drip' third shirt attracted worldwide attention on its release in 2020.

In an early example of corporate sponsorship, AC Torino were renamed Torino FIAT for 1943/44 and featured the car manufacturer's logo on their shirt.

Shirt sponsors became widespread in the 1980s, and are now a fundamental part of the design. Some partnerships, like Manchester United and Sharp (top right 1982-2000), and Borussia Dortmund and Die Continentale (bottom 1986-1997) are now firmly embedded in club history. Ajax and ABN-AMRO's 1991-2008 tie-up (right) saw the club present the sponsor vertically, whilst Fiorentina's 1997-99 shirts (top left) attract much higher prices on the vintage replica market than other shirts from that era thanks to their iconic sponsor Nintendo. Credit: Richard Kelly

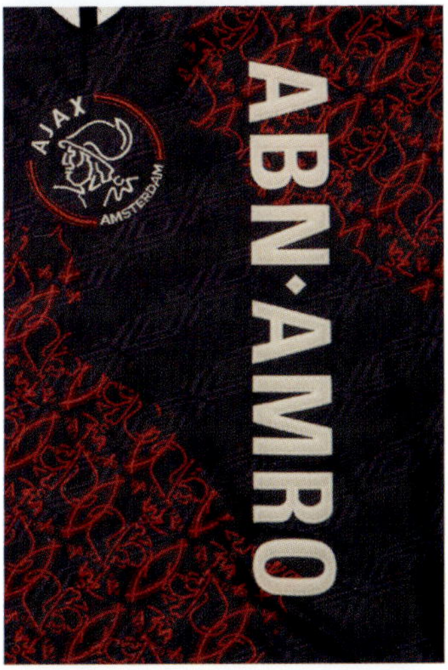

FC Barcelona's 1995-97 home shirt. Barça were one of a few teams to resist the inclusion of front-of-shirt sponsors, finally adding UNICEF's logo in 2006. Credit: Richard Kelly

Club crests began to appear more regularly on shirts in the 1970s, with some teams such as AC Milan not including their badge until the mid-1990s. Despite this, Puma's 2021/22 shirt designs were heavily criticised by fans for presenting the crest in a sublimated pattern rather than more overtly. Credit: Richard Kelly

In the 1990s, as named shirts became standard across major club and international competitions, a wider variety of memorable styles were developed. Diadora's rounded fonts used in 1994 instantly summon up an image of Roberto Baggio, 'Divine Ponytail', while the peacock blue outline of England's two-tone navy Umbro lettering in 1996 recalls the hosts' doomed bid for European Championship success on home turf. Moving into the 21st century, a black stencil font remains the mark of Real Madrid's peak *Galácticos* era, and Paris Saint-Germain's NBA-inspired digits denote their own 'megastar' phase which coincided with Nike using their Jordan sub-brand for the club. My hometown club Manchester United have used 15 different fonts since the advent of the Premier League (excluding the competition's own branded sets), and these denote different eras as effectively as the strips themselves.

Namesets were originally designed by manufacturers and clubs, with the Premier League the first to recognise the branding potential of a unified design. From 1997, clubs were required to wear the same Premier League felt lettering and numbers during league games. The style incorporates the competition's logo at the bottom of each number and has since been updated in 2007 and 2017, also changing from felt to plastic in 2013. France's Ligue 1 followed in 2008, Spain's La Liga in 2017 and USA's MLS and Italy's Serie A in 2020. The La Liga and Serie A namesets incorporated the clubs' logos rather than a league badge at the foot of the numbers. Namesets have been another source of creativity for brands, with Charly's recent Day of the Dead shirts featuring numbers made out of bone shapes. For Sweden's 2019 Women's World Cup home shirt, the numbers featured photos of female role models nominated by the players including legendary player and coach Pia Sundhage, actress Alicia Vikander, 17th-century Queen Christina and golfer Annika Sörenstam. As part of a campaign against homophobia, French Ligue 1 teams wore rainbow namesets in the final rounds of the 2020/21 season.

While surnames are most commonly used, first names and nicknames are among those to have adorned players' shirts. Johan Cruyff's son aimed to avoid his father's shadow by using his first name, Jordi, when representing the Netherlands and Manchester United, although Premier League regulations meant that he could not immediately adopt this approach on his arrival at Old Trafford. Dele (Alli), Memphis (Depay) and Bryan (Ruiz) opted for their first names to avoid representing their absent fathers' names. More happily, Alexis (Sánchez), Cédric (Soares), Jesé (Rodríguez) and Jonás (Gutiérrez) chose their first name out of preference, the latter explaining simply, 'I like my name.'

Some players have also adopted nicknames as their moniker, with Brazilians such as Pelé ('King'), Dunga ('Dopey') and Garrincha ('Little Bird') most commonly cited. Mexican striker Javier Hernández uses Chicharito ('Little Pea') after his father, known as Chícharo ('Pea') for his green eyes. Argentinian striker Sergio 'Kun' Agüero's moniker refers to a character from a Japanese cartoon in his childhood, while Givanildo 'Hulk' Vieira de Sousa goes by the superhero's name as a nickname from his father. Longer surnames have occasionally posed problems for kit men, chief among them former Dutch striker Jan Vennegoor of Hesselink. The Netherlands and Celtic both used a narrow font to ensure that his full surname would fit across the back of their shirts. However, following his move to Premier League side Hull City, the larger standard competition font did not allow this. The name could initially only be accommodated in a 180-degree curve covering most of the shirt's reverse. Similarly, Umbro had to ask for special dispensation from FIFA to use a smaller font so that the name of England's Shaun Wright-Phillips could be printed.

Another aspect to feature prominently on modern shirts is the manufacturer's logo, although this was another relatively recent addition with shirts remaining unbranded until the 1970s. French manufacturers Le Coq Sportif were the first to adorn the shirt of any team in a European Cup Final, in 1970, appearing on Feyenoord's jerseys. Umbro were the first manufacturer to include their logo on a Football League shirt, in 1973, their familiar double diamond appearing on Leeds United and Liverpool's kits. From this point, the rapid increase in kit supplier deals meant that in just four years over 90 per cent of teams would feature a logo for the first time. One exception to this was the Italian national side. The Italian Football Federation refused to allow any manufacturer logos or design elements (such as Adidas's three stripes) to be displayed during matches until 1999, although logos were included on replica versions.

At the 1981 European Cup Final, the manufacturer logo was the centre of the latest battle between Adidas and Umbro, the leading manufacturers at the time. Umbro's relationship with Liverpool had been weakened by the death of managing director John Humphreys, son of founder Harold, who had personally dealt with the club. Ambitious Adidas founder Horst Dassler was keen to secure the contract of the continent's hottest team and saw this period as his opportunity. Manufacturer logos had been permitted on club kits in UEFA competitions, Liverpool wearing the Umbro diamond in the 1977 and 1978 finals. Dassler successfully petitioned UEFA to ban shirt branding for the final, having pre-warned Adidas-sponsored finalist Real Madrid of the move. As a result, they had stitched patches over their shirts' Adidas logos – the more obvious branding of the three-stripe sleeves being permitted by UEFA. Having been unaware of this back-channelling prior to the day of the final, the Liverpool players then had to spend the pre-match period frantically covering their shirt logos with tape from the trainer's medical box. From the following season, the manufacturer's logo was permitted in all stages of the competition.

Several other embellishments have been worn on shirts over time to celebrate individual or team successes. In the 1870s, British players with regional or national representative experience would commonly have the county or national badge sewn on to their club shirt. The *scudetto* (little shield) patch featuring the Italian flag is worn by the reigning Italian league champions, having first been donned by Genoa following their 1924 championship win. Similarly, the round tricoloured *coccarda* badge has denoted the reigning Coppa Italia winners since Lazio's triumph in 1958. The tradition of national teams wearing a star above their badge to denote World Cup wins began in 1968 at the suggestion of manufacturer Athleta, when they added two stars to Brazil's shirt for a friendly match. Coach João Saldanha forbade the use of the stars at the 1970 World Cup, but having won their third trophy in Mexico it was thereafter reintroduced. The Africa Cup of Nations winners adopt a similar system for World Cup qualifiers, continental competitions and friendlies only, whereas Iraq and Qatar are the only teams to adopt stars for Asian Cup wins. Hundreds of club teams at all levels of the games have adopted stars to denote success in various regional, national and international competitions. Since 2004/05, Germany's DFB clarified their ruling that one star is awarded for a club's third Bundesliga title, a second for five, three for ten and four for 20 with Bayern Munich adding a fifth star after their 30th title win in 2021.

In the modern era, many associations have sought to promote their tournaments by way of patches or badges on the sleeve. The English Football League introduced fabric sleeve logo badges for their centenary in 1987, although they were not widely used until 1990/91. The newly established Premier League then adopted a patch featuring its own logo from 1992. Initially felt, except for some Adidas teams who suffered poor adhesion and used a fabric patch, the patches were made from plastic from 2013 onwards. From the initial design, they were made darker in 1993, and adapted with new logos in 2003 (actually two years after the main league rebrand), 2004, 2007 and 2016.

The Champions League began with black and white versions of a rectangular patch featuring the famous starball logo, the tournament name and year in its inaugural 1992/93 season. The black version was dropped for 1993/94, although returned as part of a star-shaped patch with similar detailing in 1994/95. The 1995 Champions League Final saw the first appearance of a simplified starball design, which has since been used with only minor tweaks in 1996, 2000, 2003, 2007, 2008 and 2021. A winner's patch was introduced in 2001/02, for teams who had won five or more European Cups/Champions Leagues or three in a row. Featuring a graphic of the famous trophy in an oval design, it was worn on the left sleeve and displayed the number of title wins. Initially worn by qualifying teams AC Milan, Ajax, Bayern Munich and Real Madrid, Barcelona and Liverpool have since joined this elite group. In 2021, the patch was scrapped with the number of titles integrated into the standard starball design.

For the 2018/19 season, Serie A introduced a series of annual player awards: Best Goalkeeper, Best Defender, Best Midfielder, Best Striker, Best Young Player (under the age of 23), and Most Valuable Player. The recipients of these awards were allowed to wear a pentagonal badge on their kit for the following season. Surprisingly, 2018/19 MVP winner Cristiano Ronaldo, by now of Juventus, was the only player to decide against wearing the symbol as he 'did not want to be considered above his team-mates'. By 2021/22 only two of the six previous season's winners sported the exclusive patch at any point. Gianluigi Donnarumma, Cristian Romero, Ronaldo and Romelu Lukaku had joined teams outside Italy and so were not eligible. Best Midfielder Nicolò Barella of Roma only wore his award for the first match of the season, while Fiorentina's Best Young Player Dušan Vlahović displayed his up until his mid-season move to Juventus.

Match or opponent details are now commonly included on international shirts, although the history has been quite inconsistent. England, Scotland and Wales introduced opponent names in 1950 but for all but Wales this was short-lived. Some English teams began to include matchday embroidery for finals, such as Manchester City and Manchester United adding Wembley to their crests as the location for their respective 1954 FA Cup and 1968 European Cup successes. At international level, it was not until the 1998 World Cup when branding became mandatory with teams including the wording 'FIFA World Cup France 98' on the front of their shirts either in English or French, Spanish or German equivalents. In total, 18 out of 32 sides chose English with most other teams adopting their national language, the exceptions being Romania, Bulgaria and Iran who featured the language of hosts France. This was replaced by sleeve patch branding for Euro 2000, and only a few teams such as France including the name of their opponents. England wore match details from the 2002 World Cup onwards, with teams gradually adopting the practice over the following ten to 15 years. On the club front, match embroidery was common in English finals and for English teams in European finals such as Manchester United's victorious 1991 Cup Winners' Cup and 1999 Champions League teams. Slowly other clubs began to take the same approach, starting with Valencia in the 2000 Champions League Final. For Euro 2020, which was held across multiple countries in Europe in celebration of the 60th anniversary of the tournament, Adidas teams had match details inspired by passport stamps but featuring the shape of the stadium in which each game was played.

More recently, club- or player-specific milestones have been marked with one-off details. Juventus goalkeeper Gianluigi Buffon broke the Serie A appearance record in 2020, his 648th match marked with a '648UFFON' sleeve patch. When his former Italy team-mate and Roma icon Francesco Totti made his final appearance for his hometown club after 25 seasons and nearly 800 appearances, the team wore a commemorative sleeve patch which was also made available to fans. Following the untimely death of German goalkeeper Robert Enke in 2009, the Hannover 96 players wore a patch with his squad number, 1, on their shirts for the remainder of the season to commemorate their team-mate. Borussia Dortmund's Westfalenstadion, with its imposing 'Yellow Wall' terrace, has been a key part of the club's identity since it was built for the 1972 World Cup. In February 2022 the club celebrated the milestone of playing 1,000 competitive matches in their home ground with a centralised chest patch worn during the game against Rangers. Later that year the Glasgow side, who have traditionally been associated with the Unionist community, wore a commemorative shirt detail following the death of Queen Elizabeth II.

Clubs and countries have also included symbols or modified printing in support of social or charitable causes. In the early 1980s the Corinthians team, led by midfielder Sócrates and full-back Wladimir, led a programme of activism against the military dictatorship which ruled the country from 1964 to 1985. The players adopted a democratic form of self-management, *Democracia Corinthiana*, where they would vote on matters from meal times to whether to participate in pre-match periods of squad seclusion or *concentraçãos*. This acted as a model of a possible future without the authoritarian rule of the club's owners, and in turn the government. To promote this concept, they printed the phrase 'Democracia Corinthiana' in Coca-Cola's distinctive font on the reverse of their shirts complete with blood splatter to emphasise the violent nature of the struggle. In November 1982 this message was temporarily replaced with 'Dia 15 Vote' ('Vote on the 15th') to promote voter turnout in the first multi-party elections to take place since the military takeover, which would decide the new governor of São Paulo State. The following year, the National Sporting Council banned the team from promoting their movement on their jersey as it was a political slogan. 'It seems that democracy isn't worth anything,' said Sócrates, 'not even on a shirt.' The team had appeared energised rather than distracted by their activism, winning Campeonato Paulista titles in 1982 and 1983.

More recently, after numerous prominent cases where black citizens were killed by US police in early 2020, the Premier League (where over 40 per cent of players are black) supported the Black Lives Matter campaign. When the competition resumed after the first 2020 Covid lockdown, players' names were replaced with 'BLACK LIVES MATTER' for the first 12 fixtures. The players also wore a Black Lives Matter badge and a badge supporting staff in the NHS. When the pandemic prevented supporters from attending in person, Barcelona released 15,000 *Aquí Juguem Tots* ('We All Play Here') shirts featuring the slogan as a chest detail and which fans could buy and personalise with proceeds going to charity. The shirts were then put in the stands for the match against Atlético Madrid so that supporters were represented, before being sent to the buyer.

There have been several issues when the causes supported have conflicted with the personal or religious views of players. Since 2008, many English and Scottish league clubs have worn a poppy on the front of their shirt in the run-up to Remembrance Day. James McClean – a Northern Ireland-born Catholic who plays for the Republic of Ireland – has refused to wear the symbol, citing the role of the British Army during The Troubles in his hometown. Senegal midfielder Idrissa Gueye received widespread criticism – and support – during his time with Paris Saint-Germain for refusing to wear rainbow-design numbers in support of LGBTQ+ rights for religious reasons. This follows previous examples, whereby Sevilla's Frédéric Kanouté and Newcastle United's Papiss Cissé refused to sport their clubs' gambling industry sponsors on their shirts as it conflicted with their Muslim beliefs. While Kanouté was permitted to wear an unsponsored shirt, unfortunately for Cissé photos emerged of him sat at a Newcastle casino poker table leading to a fine and withdrawal from the club's pre-season training camp.

The Manufacturer

ALTHOUGH KIT suppliers feature prominently in modern shirt designs, for the first century or so explicit branding was not permitted to promote manufacturers' wares. Many clubs were supplied by smaller, local firms, and certainly there is enough history around this topic to dedicate an entire book to it. In many cases the firms began as general clothing or sports footwear manufacturers, entering the kit world in the 1970s when the marketing potential of television, increased branding and birth of the replica market provided greater commercial opportunities. In the interests of brevity, I have focused on profiles of those firms who have supplied prominent clubs and countries in the 'branded kit' era from the 1970s onwards, incorporating their earlier origins where relevant. I would specifically highlight Stefan Appenowitz's excellent *Bundesliga Trikots 1963 bis heute* which covers German manufacturers in substantial detail.

Following Admiral's revolutionary agreement to pay Leeds United for the privilege of supplying their kit in the early 1970s, supplier contracts have progressively become a key source of revenue for leading clubs. Real Madrid's ten-year deal with Adidas is reportedly worth £110m per season from 2020, dwarfing their £60m-per-season shirt sponsorship deal with Emirates. This means that their sponsored kit alone brings in £170m annually, over 25 per cent of their £640m turnover and much greater even than total matchday revenue of £148m. This balance contrasts sharply with Manchester United's accounts from 1968/69 which were released by the Press Association in 2016. Matchday revenues for the then-European Cup holders accounted for nearly 98 per cent of all income, with televised football still in its infancy and the replica shirt boom yet to begin. As with sponsorship deals, huge discrepancies even within leagues are evident, Manchester United's £75m per season Adidas deal being 100 times that of 2020/21 Premier League rivals Sheffield United and Watford's £750,000 agreements with the same supplier.

While increased shirt sales have often been cited as the reason for high-profile transfers, the reality is that clubs make relatively little per unit in addition to their kit deal. Research by marketing analyst Peter Rohlmann in 2016 showed that out of an average £49.45 shirt sale, while the shirt itself only costs £4.79 to manufacture and ship, the retailer's (£18.13) and sportswear firm's (£12.76) cuts, VAT (£8.24), marketing costs (£1.39) and distribution (£1.17) leave clubs with £2.97. Both Real Madrid and Bayern Munich were reported to have sold over three million shirts in 2021, representing several hundred million pounds of revenue. On the manufacturer's side, direct revenue is not the only aim as football finance expert Kieran Maguire explains, 'They are looking for eyeballs for their product. You have the attention of people in 180 or more countries every time they play. It's not just the shirt, the idea is that you will go to the Adidas store and buy other products. They probably just about break even on these mega deals.'

Given the sums involved, it is not surprising that many sportswear firms are keen to develop a presence in this market. A 2014 analysis of kit suppliers of 1,061 clubs in 72 countries' top leagues by Dr Doğan Ünlücan showed 32 suppliers with more than five clubs, although 161 teams (15 per cent) wore brands with fewer than that number. Unsurprisingly, Adidas were top with 16.4 per cent of teams, with Nike (13.8 per cent), Puma (8.9 per cent) and Umbro (seven per cent), the other companies supplying more than five per cent of teams.

Bukta are one of the oldest football shirt suppliers, having been founded by father of 13 Edward R. Buck in 1879 with a primary focus on manufacturing shorts for British soldiers fighting in the Boer War. They soon branched out into other areas including sportswear, the Stockport-based firm kitting out Nottingham Forest from 1884. Bukta swiftly grew to become the leading kit supplier to UK professional football clubs, providing all the FA Cup finalists' strips throughout the 1920s and supplying more Football League teams than any other brand throughout the 1960s. They also supplied the English national team in the early 1960s including their centenary celebrations in 1963, although Umbro took over the contract prior to the 1966 World Cup triumph. Bukta continued to kit out some of the finest UK talents into the 1970s including George Best at Manchester United and Hibernian, Bobby Moore at West Ham United and Jimmy Greaves at Tottenham Hotspur. Several non-

UK clubs also sported the brand's goods, most famously Johan Cruyff's Ajax European Cup-winning teams of 1971 to 1973. Feyenoord had won the same trophy in 1970 while wearing Bukta kits, and none other than Diego Maradona donned a strip featuring the flying buck logo during a period at Sevilla in the early 1990s. The firm's popularity waned in the 1980s with the advent of greater competition, and they folded in 1992 although some teams continued to wear their strips with Leyton Orient persisting until 1994/95.

For many years, Bukta's main UK rivals were Umbro, founded by Harold Humphreys and his brother Wallace as the Humphrey Brothers Limited (hence 'um', 'bro') in 1924. Having earlier worked as a salesman for Bukta, Harold launched his own sportswear business in 1922 trading in the backroom of their parents' pub, The Bull's Head, in Mobberley, Cheshire. The company developed rapidly, breaking Bukta's stranglehold on the FA Cup by supplying both teams for the 1934 final. They showcased their wares in the nattily named 'Umbrochure' which developed from a list of available products to a full-colour publication also covering the company's background.

While Umbro and Bukta were global leaders in football kit manufacture, the lack of a replica market meant that 'mainstream' clothing manufacturers retained an interest in supplying teams. For example, the Hope Brothers shirt-tailoring firm supplied the England team in the 1940s and 1950s. As described in 'The Replica', Umbro would also develop the first dedicated replica kits in the late 1950s and were prescient in identifying the value of player endorsements to promote the brand. Figures from local club Manchester United were targeted; manager Sir Matt Busby partnered on a 'Styled by Matt Busby' range in 1959 and Scottish striker Denis Law signed an exclusive deal with the firm the following year. Busby had been the first manager to lead an English club into European competition, in 1955, which made him a good proponent of Umbro's forward-looking 'Continental' jerseys.

In part due to their innovative marketing, the company's domestic profile continued to grow, with 85 per cent of British football clubs wearing Umbro kits by the late 1960s. The firm also enjoyed international renown, supplying Brazil's 1958 World Cup-winning team (including a 17-year-old Pelé) and half of the 16 teams in the 1966 finals including victors England. Harold, described as the 'Dior of the footballing world' in a 1960s newspaper, personally visited each team in their home country ahead of the tournament. Umbro (and Bukta) relied on a network of distributors and sport shops to supply professional and amateur teams. Some suppliers would also replace the manufacturer's logo or add their own. Everton footballer and England cricketer Jack Sharp founded a sports company during his playing career, which operated independently until being taken over by JJB in the 1980s. The Jack Sharp logo appeared alongside or in place of brands such as Umbro, supplying both Everton and Liverpool as well as other teams including Wales into the 1960s.

Umbro continued to supply leading teams over the latter 20th century, including 11 of the 22 teams in the inaugural Premier League season in 1992/93. They also enjoyed a strong international presence, the same season seeing them supply Serie A's Inter Milan, Parma, Napoli and Lazio as well as other leading European clubs including Ajax and Deportivo La Coruña and soon-to-be world champions Brazil. Around the turn of the millennium their profile decreased in the face of growth from the likes of Adidas, Puma, Reebok and particularly Nike. The US firm began to supply Manchester United from 2002 and England from 2012, breaking the national team's link with Umbro which – aside from a decade with Admiral from 1964 onwards – had been in place since 1954. Nike even bought out the Manchester firm for £377m in 2008, with the company being sold on to a US brand management firm for only $225m in late 2012. Since then, Umbro have supplied a smaller pool of club and international teams including the Republic of Ireland, West Ham, Werder Bremen, Japan's Gamba Osaka and several leading Brazilian clubs.

The cosy duopoly of the British brands was broken by German firm Adidas, founded in 1924 by Adolf 'Adi' Dassler and his brother Rudolf or 'Rudi', initially as the snappy *Gebrüder Dassler Schuhfabrik* (Dassler Brothers Shoe Factory) – as the name would suggest, with footwear as their focus. Adi had made sports shoes in his mother's scullery in the small Bavarian town of Herzogenaurach since his return from the First World War. In the absence of a reliable electricity supply, the brothers sometimes had to use a bicycle to power their manufacturing equipment. The two fell out and parted company in 1948, Rudi establishing rival Puma on the other side of town while Adi set up *Adi Dassler Adidas Sportschuhfabrik*. There are various stories put forward as the reason for the split, including an affair between Rudi and Adi's wife, disagreements between the brothers' wives, and an insult made by Rudi during an Allied bombing raid in the Second World War. Alternatively, it was said that Rudi believed Adi was responsible for his wartime conscription and later arrest by the Allies.

Adidas's iconic three-stripe design was then purchased from a Finnish footwear manufacturer, Karhu Sport, in 1952 for two bottles of whisky and the equivalent of €1,600, although it would not feature on a football strip for another two decades. Other brands have since attempted to integrate their logo into shirt designs, such as Umbro's double diamond sleeve taping. However, that half a century later the three stripes are still prominently displayed on the company's shirts is a testament to the ingenious simplicity of the innovation.

Adidas supplied the West German national team's kit from 1958, but it wasn't until the early 1970s that the brand expanded their stable. Bavarian giants Bayern Munich were one of the first club sides to adopt the brand, which would also later serve as their first sponsor, with the three stripes and trefoil (invented in 1972) featuring for the first time in the early 1970s. Thereafter, the brand marks debuted on the international scene at the 1974 World Cup in Germany where 11 out of the 16 teams sported the company's strips. In the early 1970s, much of the actual manufacturing was outsourced to established suppliers like Erich Mak and Georg Schwahn as reported by Stefan Appenowitz. It was only after Adidas's purchase of Erima in 1976 that the company developed their own production capacity, initially relying heavily on the brand which would continue to supply mainly Bundesliga teams (sometimes alternating branding with Adidas) until the late 1980s.

From 1974 to 1990 Adidas supplied over half of the teams in each World Cup. On the club scene, their network grew rapidly in the 1970s to include Borussia Dortmund, Dynamo Kyiv, Marseille, AC Milan and future European Cup winners Nottingham Forest. The dominance of the UK manufacturers in British football was first challenged in 1974/75 when Adidas made Newport County's kits. Two years later, the trefoil was first seen in the top flight as Queens Park Rangers signed up with the German megabrand. The iconic logo had featured on an R's shirt in the 1975/76 squad photo, although the shirts (manufactured by then-partner Umbro) did not feature on the pitch. Adidas had previously sold boots and other equipment to UK teams via Umbro, and the Manchester firm surprisingly allowed the German giant to approach some of their clients about supplying their kit. Since the 1990s, the company has been locked in a three-way battle for club and international dominance with its hometown rival Puma and relative newcomer Nike.

Adidas's sibling company Puma was initially established as *Ruda* (Rudolf adopting a similar naming system to his brother), with the name changed to *Puma Schuhfabrik Rudolf Dassler* after a few months. Originally featuring a panther jumping through a D, the current logo has remained untouched since 1968. Designed by graphic designer Lutz Backes, the silhouette is actually of a black panther with a puma head and paws as the smaller, slighter animal made for a more aesthetically pleasing shape. Company founder Rudolf Dassler had only one criticism of the design: that the long tail would increase the size of the advert space he had to buy. Rudolf's son Armin wrote Backes a light-hearted letter to confirm their choice of design, stating, 'We only used your first draft, but we had a hearty laugh at some of your other drawings.'

Unsurprisingly, given their origins, Puma and Adidas have remained unfriendly rivals. The animosity split the small town of Herzogenaurach ('Herzo' to insiders) in which the two companies were based as effectively as the Aurach river which runs east to west across it. In this small town of around 20,000 inhabitants, there would be an employee of either firm in almost every family. Puma's headquarters were based on the north side of the town and Adidas on the south. Certain shops, bakeries, butchers and even pubs were frequented only by patrons from one side of the divide. Families were exclusively aligned to one firm or the other, openly showcasing their allegiance by their choice of clothing, while marriages across the divide were rare. Symbols of the two firms are littered throughout the town, from Puma-branded manholes to Adidas and Puma roundabouts, road names and a Puma-branded riverside running track and annual cultural festival.

Johan Cruyff did little to help the situation at the 1974 World Cup when, in contrast to his Adidas-sporting team-mates, he wore a Puma strip with two sleeve stripes attached. Puma's first entry into the football kit market was with Borussia Mönchengladbach in 1972, a relationship that lasted for two decades. In the late 1970s their roster expanded to around ten teams across Europe including Bern club Young Boys, Inter Milan, Napoli and Puma stalwart Johan Cruyff's Ajax. A decade later, their stable had doubled including leading sides FC Köln, Werder Bremen and Eintracht Frankfurt domestically, and the likes of Atlético Madrid, Valencia, Saint-Étienne and Red Star Belgrade throughout the rest of the continent. Internationally, Puma's ongoing relationship with Austria began when they supplied Germany's neighbours at the 1978 World Cup. It wasn't until the late 1990s that the company began to expand their foothold dramatically, becoming the number-one supplier at the 2006 World Cup in Germany with their 12 teams dwarfing Adidas's six. Since that point they have maintained a largely even battle with the two other sportswear giants. From the mid-1990s they have slowly developed a large market share in the club game, currently supplying leading clubs primarily in Europe including AC Milan, Borussia Dortmund, Manchester City, Marseille and Valencia.

Bukta and Umbro's grip on the UK market was also weakened by the emergence of newcomer Admiral, originally founded as underwear firm Cook & Hurst Ltd by Christopher Cook and Harold Hurst in 1908. The Admiral brand was created in 1914 and, following the 1966 World Cup, owner Bert Patrick started to manufacture football kits including subcontracting for the two larger domestic brands. As described later in 'The Replica', Admiral were the first manufacturers to use copyright legislation to protect their designs and played a key role in development of the replica kit market. Having first outfitted Leeds United in 1973, the company also supplied

England, Manchester United, West Ham United, Tottenham Hotspur and other mainly English clubs.

Despite these high-profile contracts, Admiral were declared bankrupt in 1982, although they recovered to continue to supply several leading clubs until the mid-1990s, thereafter maintaining only a small group of lower-division teams. A key reason behind their initial success was their business model, whereby they paid the club to license the team's kit rather than selling it to them. In the early deals with bigger clubs, this allowed them to make a profit, but as they began to supply lower-league clubs these sponsorship fees could not be recouped. As clubs' financial demands increased, more of these deals became unprofitable for Admiral, who unlike rivals, including Adidas and Puma, did not have substantial revenue streams from footwear and other merchandise sales which could subsidise their development.

Another UK firm which surfaced in the 1990s bear market in football kits was Reebok. Set up in 1958 in Bolton by brothers Joe and Jeff Foster as a running-shoe company, they grew rapidly to become the number-one athletics brand in the late 1980s. Having supplied Greece's kit in 1980, they signed hometown club Bolton Wanderers and international sides Russia and Ecuador in 1993. Thereafter the football division grew rapidly to take on leading European sides including Liverpool, Fiorentina, Aston Villa, Atlético Madrid and Borussia Mönchengladbach as well as the likes of Kaiser Chiefs, Palmeiras and the Chilean national team before the end of the decade. After maintaining a good stable of European and South American teams for the following decade, Reebok withdrew from the football market in the early 2010s.

Adidas and Puma's main rival for supremacy in the multibillion-dollar football apparel market is US megabrand Nike. The Portland-based firm were established in 1964 as Blue Ribbon Sports by Phil Knight, an athlete at the University of Oregon, and his coach Bill Bowerman. The company originally acted as a distributor for Japanese firm Onitsuka Tiger's running shoes, but after a fallout the company rebranded under its current name in 1971. The Nike 'swoosh' logo was designed in that year by Carolyn Davidson, a graphic design student who also took Knight's accountancy classes. Nike's first foray into football kit design was in 1978, as they supplied local North American Soccer League team Portland Timbers, thereafter signing up several more clubs in the area. Timbers' English defender Mick Hoban had retired that summer and joined Nike as soccer promotions manager. As an aside, Hoban's debut as an 18-year-old for Aston Villa was in a friendly against Santos, being presented with Pelé's shirt after the match. Keeping with the local theme, from 1983 to 1986 Sunderland became the first European team to wear Nike kit as the firm's UK distributor was based in the city.

Towards the end of the decade, the company expanded rapidly by signing European giants including Borussia Dortmund, Paris Saint-Germain, Marseille and Monaco. Further deals with Arsenal and Boca Juniors increased the brand's profile in the mid-1990s, as did their expansion into the international arena with the USA, Italy and Nigeria joining in 1995. Knight had set his eyes on securing the Brazil national team contract, stating, 'We will only truly understand football when we see the game through the eyes of Brazilians.' The following year he got his wish, and further high-profile deals with Barcelona, Inter Milan, PSV Eindhoven and Rangers, in addition to Netherlands, Portugal and Russia, saw the Portland firm start the millennium as a major force in the industry – a position they have never relinquished. Nike have also been a prominent supporter of women's football in the modern era, introducing the first bespoke women's team design in the 1995 Women's World Cup and supplying 14 of the 24 teams in the latest finals in 2019.

While never a leading name in terms of market share, French firm Le Coq Sportif was a well-recognised player in the earlier years of the replica kit industry. Formed in Romilly-sur-Seine in 1882 by Émile Camuset as a hosiery firm, they began to make sportswear in the 1920s. Then, 1955 was a breakthrough year for the company, supplying the French national side for the first time in a match against Russia, while Raymond Kopa's Stade de Reims side won their first league title wearing a Le Coq Sportif jersey. They began to supply several clubs in France and further afield in the early 1970s, including Lyon, Paris Saint-Germain, Ajax, Saint-Étienne and FC Köln. Having produced Adidas products in France under licence since 1966, a dispute with the German giants over their French operations eventually led to them buying a controlling stake in the firm. With Adidas's support, Le Coq maintained a small portfolio of high-profile club and international sides in the 1980s including Tottenham

Hotspur, Monaco, Chelsea, Inter Milan, Argentina, Italy and Spain. After the death of Adi Dassler in 1987, the firm declined thereafter largely supplying lower-division UK sides from the mid-1990s onwards.

The football kit industry is littered with several 'cult' brands beloved by hardcore kit fans. Chief among them is Danish brand Hummel, which began as Hamburg footwear firm Messmer, co-founded by shoemaker Albert Messmer in partnership with his brother Michael. Having watched players slide about on a rain-sodden pitch during a 1923 match in his hometown, Albert invented the first studded boot in an effort to improve performance in poor weather. They adopted their modern name soon after, *hummel* being the German word for bumblebee and representing how their footwear allowed the user to defy physics and move deftly. Alternatively, the explanation is that it was derived from *hummel-hummel*, a local slang greeting. Bernhard Weckenbrock took over the company in 1958, moving Hummel to the Dutch border and introducing their distinctive chevron design and bumblebee logo.

Their first foray into kit design was with second division MSV Duisburg in 1968. Having been taken over by their Danish importer in 1975, the company began to operate a small number of high-profile European club and international deals in the mid-1980s. Spanish giants Real Madrid sported the bumblebee from 1985 to 1989, while Tottenham Hotspur, Real Betis, Feyenoord, Wales and Norway were all lucky enough to don the company's distinctive designs. Hummel's most famous relationship is with the Danish national team from

1984 to 2003 and 2016 onwards, outfitting them during their shock European Championship win in 1992, having been a late replacement for Yugoslavia. The company maintained a relatively small roster of a dozen professional teams until the early 2010s, after which they expanded rapidly. Their client list at the time of writing includes clubs such as Brøndby, Everton, FC Köln, Málaga and Saint-Étienne, Japan's JEF United and a handful of leading Argentinian teams with Denmark their only international deal.

Another brand which has garnered the enduring affection of shirt fans is Italian firm Kappa, which began life as *Maglificio Calzificio Torinese* (Turin Knitted Hosiery Factory), established by Abramo Vitale in 1916. Having sent a batch of faulty socks to a customer, the company added a K and the word *kontroll* ('checked' in German) to guarantee the product's quality, and Kappa (the Italian pronunciation of K) became the new name in 1967. The company's famous Omini logo features a silhouette of a seated man and woman leaning back to back. It was created in 1969 when Abramo's grandson Maurizio Vitale (who had created clothing sub-brand Robe di Kappa the previous year) spotted the image during a photoshoot. Marketing manager Marco Boglione created the sportswear section in 1978, supplying hometown giants Juventus the following season until 2000. Kappa secured a small number of high-profile club contracts in the 1980s and 1990s including AC Milan, Sampdoria, Roma and Barcelona, expanding in the late 1990s to include AEK Athens, Red Star Belgrade, Porto, Manchester City, Real Betis and the Italian national team. They have maintained a strong presence as a second-tier firm over the past 20 years, with a primary focus on clubs rather than national teams.

While the smaller market in the 1970s and 1980s ensured that smaller firms could supply the biggest teams, the subsequent explosion left many in its wake. Ennerre was founded in 1972 by Sicilian ex-footballer Nicola Raccuglia, his initials forming the firm's badge and its name via their Italian pronunciation. The woollen shirts were initially designed and made in a convent 800m above sea level by four nuns, with the firm supplying Pescara and Lazio. Ennerre were a dominant force in Italian football in the 1980s, kitting out Fiorentina, Sampdoria, AC Milan, Roma and, most famously, Maradona's Diego Napoli during their 1987 and 1990 league titles and 1989 UEFA Cup triumph. They also supplied the Italian national team for seven matches from 1983, and several Japanese and South American teams. Raccuglia had earlier provided kit to the New York Cosmos in the late 1970s, when legendary Wales-born Italian player Giorgio Chinaglia was among their ranks. The founder left in 1985, setting up his own company, Ennedue (N2), which continued to produce and supply kits to Italian teams including Fiorentina, Atalanta, Ternana and Pescara in the late 1980s, being briefly revived to supply the latter from 2002 to 2005. The speed of Ennerre's rise was matched only by that of its demise, last supplying a Serie A team in 1991 and dropping out of football altogether by 1993.

Another iconic and short-lived Italian brand was Pouchain. Founded in 1978 by Maurizio Pouchain, who had made his fortune furnishing cruise ships and in art restoration, his eponymous and short-lived brand immediately secured a 100m Lira deal to supply Roma. Inspired by branding and merchandising in American sports, Pouchain added designer Piero Gratton's soon-to-be iconic Lupetto logo in place of the club's crest, with the company's subtle 'P' logo partnering it on the left-hand side of the chest. The firm quickly secured deals with Roma's rivals Lazio as well as Bari, Cesena, Palermo, Pescara and Udinese, also supplying them with simple, marketable logo designs. Unfortunately, their sales infrastructure could not match their design flair or scale of production and the firm withdrew from football in 1981 with a warehouse full of unsold stock.

Serie A dominated European football in the 1990s, with an Italian team featuring in all but two European and UEFA Cup finals between 1988 and 1998. As the league became one of the first to grow an international audience, many of the leading clubs sported Lotto's interlocking diamond logo. Beginning as a shoe manufacturer in Treviso in 1939, Lotto were run by the Caberlotto family who owned FC Treviso. They branched out into sportswear as Lotto Sports Italia in 1973, the logo consisting of a tennis court and football pitch superimposed on each other. Having supplied a number of smaller club and international teams including AZ Alkmaar, FC Utrecht, Cyprus and Costa Rica, Lotto added high-profile deals with Fiorentina, Atalanta and the Netherlands in 1991, with AC Milan, Bari, Napoli, Parma and Croatia joining before the company secured the Juventus contract in 2000. They have since gradually faded from most high-profile partnerships, currently maintaining a small roster of Asian and South American teams.

Lotto were joined by a series of short-lived domestic competitors in the 1990s. Founded in Veneto as a sports footwear firm in 1948 by Marcelo Danieli, Diadora's name was suggested by the founder's friend and came from a mistranslation of the Croatian town of Zadar. Entering the market in 1988 by supplying two Israeli teams, Diadora's breakthrough came after securing the kit contract for the Italian national team for the 1990 World Cup. They progressively grew a small stable of clubs including Roma, Udinese, Bologna, Boavista, Aston Villa, Fiorentina and Belgium over the following decade, declining from 2005 onwards.

Brothers Ettore and Giansevero Fila founded their eponymous clothing firm in the Piedmontese city of Biella in 1911, moving into sportswear in the 1970s. Entering the football market in 1997 with an iconic Nintendo-sponsored Fiorentina shirt, they added European and South American teams including Hamburg, Eintracht Frankfurt, West Ham United, Nacional and Cruz Azul in addition to the Scotland national team over the following five years. Maintaining a strong South American presence until 2015, the brand returned to Italian football with Vicenza in 2022.

Erreà were founded in Torrile, Italy in 1988 by Angelo Gandolfi, immediately securing the contract for Serie A Genoa thereafter adding Cagliari, Hellas Verona and Empoli in the early 1990s. They are most well known in the UK for supplying Middlesbrough, between 1994 and 2009, also kitting out Norwich City from 2011 to 2021 among a small group of mainly English and Italian teams.

As with the Italian league, in the early years of the replica market smaller firms challenged the growing global giants in many countries only to fade as the market moved beyond the reach of national brands. The burgeoning football shirt market in Spain was dominated by Mont-Halt, founded by Agustí Montal, who served as Barcelona's president from 1969 to 1977. As reported by BenditosColores on Twitter, the company's products were often rebranded by other firms such as Valencia supplier World Sports or by the company's distributors such as Deportes Cóndor who held a contract with Atlético Madrid. They supplied several Spanish sides including Barcelona, Sevilla and Real Madrid throughout the 1970s, thereafter fading from prominence.

Similarly, beloved brand Meyba was founded in Barcelona in the 1940s by José Mestre and Joaquín Ballbé (hence 'Me-y-Ba') as a sportswear firm. They entered the professional football market in some style, securing the contract for Barcelona in 1980 which they held for ten years. In the same decade they supplied several top Spanish teams including Real Betis, Atlético Madrid, Racing Santander and Real Valladolid. However, they faded quickly after the Barcelona contract ended in 1992, falling bankrupt in 1994 and closing in 1997. The company's rights were purchased in 2013 and from 2020 they supplied FC Twente's kits under creative director Neal Heard. Designer Heard had previously worked on crossover collections between fashion and football for Le Coq Sportif and Lyle & Scott, and had also written *The Football Shirts Book*, published in 2017, which celebrated football shirt design and culture.

Into the 1990s, smaller firms and even those without a football or even sporting background were still able to establish a presence in the Spanish top flight. For 1990/91, Real Zaragoza wore kits from Mc Yadra, a Madrid-based school uniform manufacturer who had been established less than a decade. Another modern entrant to the Spanish market was Kelme, established as a footwear firm in Elche by Diego and José Quiles in 1963 and who began to focus on sportswear from 1983. The first football kit to feature their paw-mark logo was that of the Colombian national side in 1993. The following year, they secured the contract to supply Real Madrid for four years, with *Los Blancos* winning two La Liga titles and the Champions League wearing the Spanish firm's strips. Torino, Real Valladolid, Real Mallorca, Villarreal and Argentina's Club Atlético Lanús were signed up before the end of the decade. The brand ran into financial difficulties in 2003, requiring a €9m credit line from the Valencian government. Following a takeover in 2008, the brand began a steady resurgence such that in 2018/19 they outfitted more Spanish top-flight sides than any other company.

Compatriot firm Joma was founded as a shoemaker in 1965 by Fructuoso López, with the name taken from Fructuoso's oldest son José Manuel (hence Joma). They entered the market in 1990 supplying Real Betis's strip, thereafter maintaining a small stable of mostly Spanish sides in addition to a handful of international and European club sides including Atalanta and Sampdoria. Most notable are their partnerships with Real Vallecano from 1994 to 2005 and Sevilla from 2001 to 2011.

While European firms dominated the market initially, several US companies have joined compatriot Nike in supplying the 'soccer' boom. Pony (Product of New York) was founded in 1972 by Roberto Muller with financial support from Adi Dassler's son (and Adidas chairman) Horst. Originally a sports footwear firm, they first supplied Paris Saint-Germain in 1977. Having provided kits to a handful of teams including Borussia Dortmund, Lyon, and the Mexican national side in the 1980s, the firm joined the flood of growing brands in the 1990s. They secured contracts with Southampton, West Ham United, Tottenham Hotspur and Coventry City in the burgeoning English Premier League, and Dundee United, Hearts and Motherwell north of the border in addition to several Mexican league teams. Following a takeover by entertainment group The Firm, Pony announced their withdrawal from football in 1998, thereafter only surfacing to provide the Catalonia national team strip in 2014.

More short-lived was the involvement of US brand Champion, who began life in 1919 as the Knickerbocker Knitting Company under founders the Feinbloom Brothers. Having supplied US teams in other sports since shortly after their foundation, their first foray into association football was supplying the New York Cosmos in 1975 and 76. Thereafter, they were not part of the explosion in football kits, turning up again only in 1999 to provide Serie A's Parma for the following six seasons. A four-year spell supplying Sochaux from 2001, two years from 2008 as Wales's kit manufacturer and a solitary season at Wigan Athletic in 2008/09 were their only other forays into the beautiful game.

A more recent high-profile success story is that of New Balance. Founded in 1906 in Boston, USA the footwear firm began supplying kits to Argentinian clubs in the late 1990s. In 2016 they expanded dramatically, securing the Liverpool, Celtic, Porto, Lille and Sevilla contracts, and they have subsequently added the likes of Roma, Bilbao's Athletic Club and the Republic of Ireland.

Set up in Washington, D.C. in 1996 as the first manufacturer of underlayer garments, Kevin Plank's Under Armour firm have supplied European and South American teams including Tottenham Hotspur, Aston Villa, Southampton, St. Pauli and São Paulo since entering the market with Hannover 96 in 2008.

Despite the Japanese football market being generally relatively insular, as detailed in 'The Replica', the country's firms began to make an impact abroad in the 1990s. Beginning as Kobe sports footwear firm Onitsuka Tiger (later to be embroiled in a spat with what would become Nike) in 1949 under founder Kihachiro Onitsuka, the ASICS (*anima sana in corpore sano* – 'a sound mind in a sound body') Corporation was formed in a merger in 1977. Having supplied the Japanese national side in 1979 (which they would do intermittently over the next two decades), from 1989 they expanded on the club front. Sampdoria, Roma, Borussia Mönchengladbach, Bordeaux and Atalanta were recruited, in addition to Newcastle United, Leeds United, Aston Villa and 1995 Premier League winners Blackburn Rovers. They maintained a smaller stable of mainly Italian clubs including Torino, Genoa, Cagliari and Lecce over the following decade, thereafter continuing to supply hometown club Vissel Vobe as they have done since 1998.

ASICS' main domestic rival is Mizuno, whose name Japanese football expert Alan Gibson revealed is commonly mispronounced by western sports fans (the second syllable should not be emphasised). Founded in 1906 in Osaka, Japan, they supplied kits to all ten J.League teams from its foundation in 1993 until 1995. Having picked up several English teams including Port Vale, Reading and Scunthorpe United in the late 1990s (and Fiorentina for 2001/02), the company predominately supplied Japanese teams until re-entering the European market with Lazio and VfL Bochum in 2022.

The European giants have long been regular suppliers of both national and club sides in South America, but several domestic firms have also previously clothed the continent's greatest teams. In Brazil, Athleta (formed in 1935 in São Paulo by Antonio Pádua de Oliveira) supplied the Brazilian national team from 1953 to 1977, Brazilian clubs including Corinthians, São Paulo, Santos, Palmeiras and Flamengo, as well as Benfica, Pelé's New York Cosmos and the Paraguay national team. Corinthians were the first club to don Athleta gear with overt branding in the 1960s; while regulations banned branding on matchwear, the company mark was included on training gear. As recounted to globo.com by Oliveira's grandson Antonio Bulgarelli, the company's factory became a meeting place for players who – a world away from today's multimillion-pound sponsorships – would pose for free for promotional images. Athleta and clubs operated in true partnership, the company offering training and matchwear for free, taking their revenue from replica shirts and fashion wear. In return, clubs would bring shirts back from matches against foreign teams so that the manufacturer could gain insight on new materials, detailing, etc. Such was Pelé's importance to the firm that they broke this arrangement and insisted that he accept a VW Beetle as a gift which he gave to his father. The firm had disappeared by the early 1980s due to pressure from international firms but was re-founded in 2009 and now supplies several lower-league Japanese teams.

Dell'Erba were another Brazilian marque to emerge in the 1980s, having manufactured sportswear for other brands including Athleta since the 1950s. According to the family, they supplied Athleta with shorts for the Brazil national teams from 1954 to 1974 and manufactured Topper's Brazil shirts from 1982 to 1990. Certainly, Topper club strips including those of Corinthians were manufactured by the firm and carried a Dell'Erba collar label. Ricardo Dell'Erba son of the firm's founder Sérgio, began making unlicensed replicas of European shirts in the 1980s but from 1988 the firm supplied its own designs. Taking substantial inspiration from European shirt designs, particularly those of Umbro, Dell'Erba created strips with bold sublimated patterns for the likes of Atlético Mineiro, Santos and Portuguesa in the early 1990s. The professionalisation of the Brazilian kit market in the mid-1990s meant that smaller firms could not afford the large contract fees and Dell'Erba withdrew in 1996, eventually being declared bankrupt in 2010.

Two other South American manufacturers which retain the affections of football shirt fans are Penalty and Topper.

Penalty (formed in 1970 in São Paulo by Grupo Campucci) were originally famous as a ball manufacturer, but began to supply leading Brazilian teams including Grêmio, Fluminese, Santos, Botafogo, São Paulo and Atlético Mineiro in the 1980s. Weathering the 1990s professionalisation of the market, they maintained a healthy group of leading teams until around 2015, thereafter primarily supplying Japanese teams. Argentinian brand Topper was founded in 1975 as a trainer manufacturer by leading textile maker Alpargatas (founded 1885), with the company's name being that of president Eduardo Oxenford's dog. Beginning in the late 1970s, Topper have since supplied leading Argentinian and Brazilian clubs including River Plate, Boca Juniors, Independiente, Cruzeiro, Corinthians and Santos, also securing the Brazil national team contract from 1982 to 1990.

Although overshadowed by their compatriots Adidas and Puma, other German firms briefly shone in the 1990s kit boom. Uhlsport were established in 1948 in the south of the country, originally supplying football equipment such as goalkeeper gloves, shin guards, footballs and boot studs. They entered the shirt market in the late 1980s, securing contracts with the likes of Inter Milan, Bologna, Fiorentina, Kaiserslautern, Freiburg, Auxerre and Croatia. In addition, they specifically provided goalkeeper shirts to the likes of Borussia Dortmund and Juventus while outfield players would wear the contracted brand. While they were soon priced out of the high-profile club deals, they continued to supply several European teams, at the time of writing. Similarly, Reusch were founded as a glove manufacturer by Karl Reusch but supplied teams including VfL Bochum, Hertha Berlin, St. Pauli, KFC Uerdingen 05 and Wolfsburg in the 1990s, retaining a supply to several South American sides thereafter.

The depth of the English football pyramid means that suppliers of lower-league sides have also attracted admirers. Scoreline had a short-lived run supplying English league teams including Fulham, West Ham United, Norwich City, Leicester City and Wolverhampton Wanderers between 1987 and 1991. Similarly, Ribero supplied others in the early 1990s, including Coventry City, Crystal Palace and Norwich during the inaugural Premier League season in 1992/93. Between 1986 and 1996, Matchwinner provided striking designs to the likes of Bournemouth, Swansea City, Greenock Morton, Hull City and Bolton Wanderers. Sports manufacturer Gola were founded in Leicester in 1905, and had a brief spell as supplier for Huddersfield Town, Barnsley, Blackpool and Stockport County from 1991 to 1993. Founded in India by a Mr Sondi, Sondico produced football equipment including teamwear after relocation to Manchester. The firm have supplied a small number of professional clubs including FC Twente, Portsmouth, and Sheffield Wednesday since 2012.

The boom in interest in football kits over the last decade has brought new players into the market, with Manchester firm Castore the most successful. It was founded in 2015 by brothers Phil and Tom Beahon, who had been talented sportsmen but unable to break into the top professional sides in football and cricket respectively. Instead, they retired from sport and entered the finance world to raise money to fund a sportswear firm. Having visited manufacturers across Europe to learn about the industry, they signed up Rangers in 2020 and have since seen a meteoric rise adding clubs including Newcastle United, Wolverhampton Wanderers, Aston Villa, Bayer Leverkusen, Sevilla, Feyenoord and Genoa. However, their rapid expansion has led to production issues such as club crests and the Castore logo being applied to replica shirts upside down. In addition, in August 2022 Newcastle were forced to wear a warm-up shirt with additional branding for their match against Brighton as all three of their standard Castore kits clashed with the south coast team's strip.

For a long time, distinctive custom design shirts were largely the preserve of top professional clubs, with amateur and semi-professional teams doomed to a life clad in uninspiring big-brand templates and low-quality teamwear. Manchester-based firm Hope and Glory are one of the few manufacturers to offer bespoke kits at low volume and prices. Owner and chief designer Ric Dennis likes to incorporate unique aspects of a team's culture into the design in the form of 'Easter egg' features.

Oldham Athletic fan Ric, a graphic designer by trade, first moved into shirt design in 2014 when his club were disappointed with the options offered by their supplier. The club accepted Ric's offer to work with the manufacturer, and this experience led to him setting up a company offering bespoke kit design service to smaller clubs. In a break with tradition, Hope and Glory do not offer template designs, with each strip designed from scratch. The jade and gold away kit designed for North

Ferriby came sixth in the National Football Museum's 2020/21 Nation's Greatest Shirt exhibition ahead of designs from the likes of Manchester United. The same shirt was rated the top non-league shirt and 20th overall in world football by Footy.com readers. Like many manufacturers, Hope and Glory are also aware of their social responsibilities and have offered clubs the opportunity to use EcoKit fabric made from recycled plastic bottles in their kits since 2020.

On the international front, smaller European nations have gained access to custom kits through UEFA's Kit Assistance Scheme. Launched in 2007, the venture sees UEFA members given free training and matchwear for their senior and under-21 teams in addition to participating in the development of the bespoke garments and equipment. As of 2022, Italian firm Erreà were supplying Andorra, Belarus, Cyprus, Faroe Islands, Kazakhstan, Liechtenstein, Luxembourg, Malta and San Marino. The first shirts to emerge from the new partnership demonstrated a variety of nation-specific features made possible through access to the company's design teams. Broad, bold zig-zags in the national flag colours were emblazoned on Andorra's home shirt, while an outline of the Faroe Islands was printed on their third shirt. A Maltese cross formed a repeating pattern on Malta's home and away strips, with a huge version of the San Marinese federation crest sublimated into their home jersey. The ability for players and fans to wear a distinctive shirt is key to a strong feeling of identity with the national side. San Marino's Andrea Zoppis said, 'The Kit Assistance Scheme is very important for a little federation like us and all the smaller associations. It gives us the commercial power that without this scheme we don't have ... The opportunity to create a new journey is emotional – we choose some elements that are connected to the history of our country and we are proud of it.'

Clubs have increasingly reached out to high-end fashion houses for collaborative projects. In 2014, Real Madrid released an iconic third shirt featuring a subtle, intricate dragon graphic by Japanese fashion designer Yohji Yamamoto. In 2021 they released another collaborative kit sponsored by Yamamoto's Adidas Y-3 sub-brand to celebrate the brand's 20th anniversary, at an eye-watering price of £160. Coinciding with the club's 120th anniversary, the shirt was worn only in one *El Clásico.* In 2018, Nike signed a four-year deal with Paris Saint-Germain to supply the club's shirts through their Jordan sub-brand. The shirts featured the brand's Jumpman logo in place of the swoosh, and incorporated design features from basketball, notably from Michael Jordan's successful Chicago Bulls era. The following year Juventus announced a collaboration with high-end skateboard brand Palace. This was followed in short succession by collaborations with Adidas stablemates Arsenal, Manchester United and Real Madrid to release fourth shirts designed by musician Pharrell Williams under his Adidas HUMANRACE brand featuring reworked versions of the clubs' classic kits. In 2021, Napoli followed by collaborating with Milan-based designer Marcelo Burton to release a limited-edition kit worn in a Serie A game against Inter Milan and featuring his trademark bird design across the shoulders. They went one step further the following season, signing fashion brand Emporio Armani as their official kit supplier, although it appeared that the EA7-branded kits were still made by previous supplier Kappa.

While most clubs are free to negotiate their own kit supplier, since 2004 Adidas have acted as the official supplier to all Major League Soccer teams. Some teams already under contract wore other brands until 2006, but since then all sides in the competition have sported the three stripes. Initially a ten-year deal worth $15m per season, the league's growing profile and size was illustrated by the six-year deal signed in 2017 worth $117m annually. Similarly, the new J.League competition adopted Mizuno as sole supplier at its launch in 1993. Clubs with existing suppliers wore other brands in the Emperor's Cup competition, with replica versions of the J.League kits featuring the team name rather than the sponsor's logo worn on the pitch.

Finally, several clubs have taken matters into their own hands and designed kits in-house, either due to a manufacturer bankruptcy or the conviction that greater revenue could result from cutting out the middleman. In this vein, Borussia Dortmund set up Goool.de in 2000, manufacturing their own kit until 2008 and also supplying other sides including second-tier Dynamo Dresden and Kickers Offenbach. Southampton (1999–2008 and 2014/15) and Leicester City (Fox Leisure, 1992–2000) have also manufactured their own kits for an extended period, as have St. Pauli through brands Do You Football? (2005–2014) and D!Y (2021 to date). Chelsea (1986/87), Real Betis (1992–1994, 2009–2012), Athletic Club (2003–2009), Roma (2013/14), Sheffield Wednesday (Elev8, 2017–2021) and

Royale Union Saint-Gilloise (Union Soixante, 2022 to date) are among those to have also produced in-house designs.

In a slight twist on own-brand kits, the Japanese FA produced their own strips with Puma, Adidas and ASICS branding during the 1990s as described in detail by Lucas Santos on the Museum of Jerseys website. Having worn a series of staid template designs and cycling almost annually between the three manufacturers in the 1980s, the FA commissioned a design inspired by the wing of the FA's crow emblem and typical of the bold geometric patterns popular at that time. The blue home shirt, partnered by a white away top with inverted colours, first appeared as an Adidas trefoil-branded version at the 1992 Asian Cup. Puma and ASICS versions followed in the next two years, with the branding of the same design continuing to cycle between the three. A second shirt with dramatic flame designs on the sleeves first appeared with ASICS branding during the 1996 Olympics in Atlanta. Following the usual cycle, the shirt made its final bow at the 1998 World Cup with the nation qualifying for the tournament for the first time. While ASICS made the senior team jersey, Adidas and Puma shared responsibility for Japan's age-group teams. From 1998, Adidas have had sole responsibility for supplying the nation's kits.

The Replica

TECHNICALLY, REPLICA shirts have almost always been available to football fans. From the emergence of dedicated sportswear brands in the late 19th century, jerseys were typically bought by the dozen from local sports shops. However, they were marketed solely to players with no suggestion that a fan would wish to emulate their heroes' attire. The first dedicated replica shirts were produced by Umbro in 1959, as part of a 'full kit' package only available in child sizes. Pointedly, they were marketed as Umbroset for Boys with no equivalent available for girls. While these sold well enough, the simplicity of designs, the lack of trademarks and their interchangeability – particularly in the 1960s – meant that it was not possible to buy a shirt unique to a chosen club.

Bert Patrick of Admiral would soon change this, inspired by the passing of the Copyright Act in 1968 which would allow clubs to protect their identity. Admiral signed their first professional deal with Leeds United in 1973, being the first supplier to pay a club for the rights to design and supply their kit. By creating a custom, copyrighted design and adding the Admiral logo, the only way a child could obtain an authentic shirt was through Admiral. The following year they added the England team to their stable, paying the same £10,000 figure as with their Leeds contract in return for a per cent cut in revenue. *Roy of the Rovers* illustrator Paul Trevillion had pitched the idea of branded replica shirts to Umbro around the same time, but the company was unconvinced that a product pitched at children could raise substantial revenue.

The early replica kits were still lacking in some authentic details, including plastic club badges which rarely survived more than a few washes intact. These were different from the embroidered details of the player-issued shirts, a theme that would continue across the replica shirt era. Admiral also received criticism for the shirts' high price, as when Manchester United signed with the firm in 1975 their £15 kits were three times the price of the previously unbranded replicas. Despite this, Admiral shirts were a big seller, and firms such as Umbro, Bukta and Adidas joined an arms race, with 84 of the 92 Football League clubs displaying a manufacturer's logo just four years after the first branded shirt. Admiral also led promotional ventures by debuting new shirts in high-profile games such as West Ham's 1976 European Cup Winners' Cup Final, while later the final home match of the season would be used to drum up anticipation for the mid-summer launch. The boom-and-bust story of Admiral is worth much more time and attention than that permitted within this book. Andy Wells's book *Get Shirty: The Rise & Fall of Admiral Sportswear* is a fantastic in-depth history of the brand, informed by interviews with key figures from the company and the wider footballing world. It arose from an ITV documentary of the same name, although at the time of writing the TV programme is not available online.

Having previously been promoted solely as sports equipment, in the late 1970s adverts began to show children's replica shirts presented as everyday wear. The shirts were still exclusively marketed to children, although photographic investigations by Dr Chris Stride from the University of Sheffield have since shown pictures of young adults squeezed into the largest youth-sized shirts at the 1974 and 1976 FA Cup finals. This was around the time that adult-sized shirts began to be released, being spotted at Liverpool's 1977 European Cup Final and among Scotland fans at a British Home Championship match the same year. However, with few exceptions their uptake was limited until the end of the 1980s. Dr Stride attributes this to several factors, including the poor reputation of football fans at the time making self-identification as a supporter neither desirable nor safe for most people. At that time the clubs lacked merchandising infrastructure, while national sport-shop chains were also in their infancy so there was limited marketing and availability for adult fans. During this period, there was an explosion in shirt sponsorship, although at first these were not supplied on replica kits. They then became available at extra cost, before becoming incorporated as standard in the late 1980s.

Towards the end of the 1980s, the public perception of football and its supporters in the UK began to improve. Indie music bible *New Musical Express* declared football to be 'hip again', while uber-cool Manchester band New Order wore England replica shirts in the music video for their 1990 World

Cup song 'World in Motion'. Cool Britannia icon Kate Moss made her magazine-cover debut in the May 1990 issue of culture magazine *The Face* as part of an article on the upcoming World Cup in Italy (another event which catapulted football back into the mainstream). Dr Stride and his colleagues showed that this change in public perception was mirrored by an increase in replica shirts at games, the proportion of fans wearing them increasing tenfold to 30 per cent between the 1986/87 and 1993/94 seasons.

Clubs began to recognise the potential for replica shirts as a source of revenue and broadened their marketing and product range. In the late 1980s, adverts for replica shirts began to show adults who were not players dressed in the kit for the first time. In addition, the range of available sizes increased, and the larger shirts were enthusiastically bought by older fans. This was illustrated in a January 1993 article in *The Observer*, where Umbro's marketing director Peter Draper reported extra-large shirts as being the most popular size. Appealing to a broader market of both men and women was essential to justify the exponential rise in kit supplier contract fees, Umbro paying Manchester United £10m over six years from 1992. The rise in club superstores and mail order, in addition to the explosion in high-street sport shops such as Allsports and JJB Sports who had 120 stores by 1994, improved availability of replica strips. In 2003, a cartel of sportswear retailers and leading football clubs were fined £18.6m for colluding with the manufacturer to fix the price of replica Umbro shirts from teams including England, Manchester United, Chelsea, Celtic and Nottingham Forest.

Retailer JJB received the largest fine of £8.4m, with Umbro paying £6.6m, Manchester United £1.6m and the English FA £158,000. Umbro had insisted that partners sold shirts at pre-agreed prices, with those who refused being removed from approved supplier lists.

Price fixing of shirts was yet another example of Premier League clubs aiming to maximise the money extracted from fans. From rising ticket prices to the need to sign up to multiple expensive TV services to access all televised games, the huge financial growth of the English top tier has come largely at the direct expense of domestic match-going and armchair fans. Unfortunately, as outlined in the previous chapter, shirt-related revenues have become more important than matchday income for leading sides. In addition, they require little in the way of infrastructure or other investment from the club's side with most of the risk falling on the manufacturer. Considering that clubs like Tottenham Hotspur are willing to invest up to £1bn in new stadia to increase matchday income, it seems very unlikely that they will give up the reliable, regular cash injections that shirt revenues provide. Therefore, replica jerseys with production, marketing and distribution costs totalling less than £10 will continue to retail for £70 to £100 or more. In addition, the annual release of home, away, third and 'special' shirts which feeds this revenue stream will almost certainly be maintained despite its cost to consumers and the environment.

Replica jerseys in women's sizes emerged for some teams around the turn of the millennium but were not produced across all teams. Since that point, issues such as shirt cut and availability have been a consistent problem for female fans. In 2014/15, Adidas's Manchester United home shirt was criticised for having a low-cut, revealing neckline, but a similar style was still being used for Real Madrid's shirts in the 2018/19 season. When the Welsh men's national team qualified for Euro 2016, their first major tournament in 58 years, female supporters were stunned to discover that Adidas would not produce a shirt for them despite doing so for other sides in the tournament including Germany, Spain and Sweden. Adidas also did not produce Premier League side Wolverhampton Wanderer's replica shirts in women's sizes during the three years they held a contract with the club from 2018 to 2021. Nike are also not exempt from embarrassing errors, having initially only made the new Australian women's side available in men's replicas at launch in 2020 with a plan to introduce women's sizes two years later. To promote the upcoming 2022 Women's European Championship, Spain, Belgium and Germany's men's teams wore the women's team shirt in men's sizes in friendlies leading up to the tournament. The men's player-issue shirts had features such as heat-applied logos not available to their female counterparts. Even two decades on from the birth of this market, coverage remains incomplete with major sides missing women's versions of men's shirts and vice versa, while few clubs make the player versions of these shirts available despite male fans of the men's teams being able to buy them.

One of the challenges to the income stream provided by shirts is the rise in counterfeit items, which have emerged as a cheap but illegal alternative to expensive official merchandise.

This situation has a parallel in the rise of unlawful TV streaming services, which have grown rapidly in the face of increasing subscription costs and the fragmentation of TV packages. Nowadays, the big brands have global networks working to identify and prevent unlicensed production of their shirts. In addition, their supply chains reach into the farthest corners of the world. In the 1980s, this infrastructure was not in place and in the absence of local official suppliers even legitimate brands took the opportunity to reproduce the big clubs' designs. In addition to supplying top-flight Brazilian clubs, Dell'Erba reproduced and sold copies of European teams' shirts including AC Milan and Napoli. Retaining the shirt's colour scheme, club badge and even sponsor, the Dell'Erba 'D' logo replaced the original supplier.

Ben Houston, director of Back Four Brand Protection, gave some insights into the counterfeit shirt industry. He set up his company in 2011 having worked in brand protection for the likes of Nike and Manchester United, and they provide these services for around 60 teams and manufacturers. 'The scale is incredible now compared to 20 years ago,' Ben explained. 'At that time in the UK outlets wouldn't sell counterfeit football shirts and only low-quality products were available abroad. Now UK consumers want high-quality versions, so they can wear them at the match without being mocked.' There are now hundreds of factories, mainly in the Far East, which produce these fake strips. The increasing global interest in the Premier League has fuelled this market, with the Covid-19 pandemic and subsequent cost-of living-crisis also boosting demand for these cheaper replicas.

'These factories have all the technology that the major brands do,' said Ben. 'Once a kit is released, or even when images of the kit are leaked pre-release, the factories can mock up a version in days.' He dismissed a popular urban myth peddled by consumers and manufacturers that the counterfeiters buy or produce the shirts in the same factories as genuine items. To the trained eye the shirts are not identical, and mistakes or poor-quality implementations of badges or stitching are obvious close-up.

Current resources mean that elimination of all of the counterfeit suppliers is not possible, and the aim of brand protection teams is to suppress the market supply by making life difficult for counterfeit trade and preventing products from getting to consumers. Most manufacturers have in-house brand protection teams who work with police, trading standards, customs, etc. to seize as much fake product as possible. They will conduct raids in factories abroad, and order removal of websites or social media accounts offering the counterfeit goods. In addition, they aim to suppress demand by educating consumers about investing in official products.

Ben addressed the idea that for parents in particular, the idea of spending a fraction of the price on a similar-looking garment could seem like a no-brainer. 'There are lots of good reasons in addition to legality to avoid buying counterfeit goods,' he explained. 'If you buy these goods, you don't know the working conditions under which they're produced or who is working there. There are safety issues as you have no idea what materials are being used or which substances are applied in production and whether they're harmful or not. Clubs are missing out on revenue which pays staff and so is reinvested into communities, and a chunk of the cost is VAT paid to government. It's not only large clubs, we have recently seen counterfeit goods from all Championship clubs. Many of them face challenging financial situations, and thus the sales of official merchandise are crucial. In addition, for the consumer they are poor quality, don't last and as a byproduct that harms the brand image for the manufacturer.'

Returning to official products, the term 'replica' has always been slightly misleading, as from Admiral's earliest custom branded kits the version offered to fans has differed from that worn on the pitch by their heroes. Initially these differences were quite subtle, as supporter kits had a cheaper plastic or felt badge rather than the embroidered version seen on the players' shirts. Another important consideration is that many kits over the last 50 years of the replica era have only been made available commercially in short-sleeved versions, particularly for teams in warmer climates. In the 1980s and early 1990s, some clubs only made home strips available for sale, Nike's series of four stunning Borussia Dortmund away shirts from 1990 to 1994 by designer Drake Ramberg being a well-known example of tops that were unavailable as replicas.

When intricate jacquard patterns became common in the 1990s, manufacturers such as Lotto and Puma offered 'basic' versions without the jacquard and with the club and brand logos sublimated into the fabric rather than being rendered in felt or embroidered. As player namesets were introduced, manufacturers including *El Clásico* club suppliers Kappa and

Kelme sublimated these details (and the La Liga sleeve patch) within the player version of the shirt although others offered this as part of the standard fan version. A good example of the latter is Italian manufacturer Galex's 1998/99 Perugia shirt which sold in huge quantities with Japanese megastar Hidetoshi Nakata's name and number 7 embedded within the silky red polyester on the reverse.

Originally, namesets were priced according to the amount of numbers and letters used, meaning that fans of Manchester United's number 14 Andrei Kanchelskis had to fork out more than double that of Paul Ince, who wore 8. Some of the original older Premier League stock is still available on auction sites. The letter R inevitably goes out of stock first presumably due to its heavy use in star names such as Shearer, Rooney, Henry and Terry, and often with the older namesets buyers are left to puzzle out which less popular former stars they can recreate from the few characters remaining. Looking at one 1999–2007 Premier League eBay listing, the available Lextra brand felt letters were B, C, D, H, I, J, L, M, Q, U and Y, which gives an idea of the challenge. UEFA regulations impacted on the size and detail of sponsors in addition to manufacturer branding for clubs involved in European competition, with the replica versions usually sold with the original configuration.

As brands introduced performance-focused designs from the late 1990s, some of the features were reserved for player versions to keep costs down. While 2002 World Cup players benefitted from Nike's dual-layer Cool Motion technology, those in the terraces were left to sweat it out in a single-layer version. Bonded polyester replaced sewn seams in match shirts, with laser-cut ventilation holes also reserved for players. The early 2000s also saw a reversal of the approach to badges and other adornments. Whereas previously embroidered versions had been reserved for the higher-spec player-issue versions, these were now more commonly used for fan strips. Due to weight considerations and the aim for 'zero distraction', players would now sport plastic printing of these features. Similarly, inside the shirt the potential irritation of washing tags (which many players and fans cut out) was removed from the player strips by printing the details on the shirt itself. Fan versions would now feature a looser fit more friendly to the average physique of a non-athlete.

Player version or 'authentic' shirts are available at a premium price, typically 20 to 30 per cent more than the fan release. There is also an added layer of complexity, with these authentic shirts having small differences from the version supplied to a team for match use. For example, Adidas kit-room stock typically uses a number-based size system rather than medium, large, etc. Some specialist retailers such as Classic Football Shirts can source this stock and offer it as kit-room stock. It is not only the shirt itself that differs, but typically larger player-specific printing is used to aid on-pitch visibility. For example, Premier League sleeve patches are 80mm wide for players and 65mm wide for fan shirts with numbers measuring 258mm and 230mm high respectively.

In addition to featuring new technologies into player strips to improve performance, the advent of the internet and later social media saw features aiming to incorporate these and other new technologies into more interactive replica shirt designs. French side Lyon's 2012/13 home strip incorporated a 3D pattern on the front, with the effect only visible to viewers wearing 3D glasses which were supplied with the replica version. In 2018, Nike incorporated their Near-Field Communication-based NikeConnect technology into the Chelsea third shirt. This allowed owners to scan the shirt and access unique products and content in the Nike smartphone app. Less successfully, it allowed fans to input into the design of a 'Chelsea Shirtholders Kit', the results of which could charitably be described as 'unique'. Southampton's 2021/22 Hummel-branded home shirt was embedded with augmented reality technology so that fans could scan parts of the shirt to unlock features such as a 3D image of midfielder James Ward-Prowse and a portal allowing supporters to virtually browse the club's St Mary's Stadium through their phone screen. In the same year Fiorentina released 95 limited-edition shirts based on the controversial non-fungible token technology. This allowed the shirt's ownership to be tracked and transferred electronically thanks to a smart patch on the front.

Aside from the differences between the various player- and fan-level kits, another source of variation is in regional versions of replica strips across the globe. Factors such as import restrictions mean that some international firms license production to local companies. For example, in the first 30 years of the replica industry many kits in Argentina were supplied by local firm Gatic. Eduardo Bakchellian had set up the company in 1953, becoming the licencee for Adidas products in Argentina in 1969. They later held licenses for sportswear by other high-profile international companies including Umbro, New Balance, ASICS and Le Coq Sportif. By 1995, Gatic employed over 8,000 people across 19 factories and had a turnover of ~$350m.

Gatic took some creative licence with the reconstruction of original designs, with collars and other details differing from the European replica versions. As an example of this practice, the 1988 Netherlands shirt featured in at least seven versions in different territories, although in some cases the differences were very subtle. Taking the original match-worn versions as a reference, the UK version was distinguished by a lion crest without the federation's KNVB abbreviation. Over in the Republic of Ireland, the 'fish scale' pattern was separated into individual triangles and parallelograms by thick black lines in contrast to the standard subtle grey/silver marks. South American versions with different collars featured a deeper orange shade, while a West German version was available with a stitched badge without the monogram. Other, more subtle, differences were evident with West German and Japanese versions chiefly distinguished by the differing-sized label designs.

Relaxation of the ban on Chinese-made products and Argentina's economic difficulties saw Gatic fall on hard times around the millennium. Adidas products accounted for 70 per cent of the firm's turnover, and the German giant's decision not to renew Gatic's exclusive licensing contract in 2002 sounded its death knell with the final closure occurring by 2004.

Founded in 1935, DESCENTE performed a similar role in the Japanese market. They gained the trademark rights for

Le Coq Sportif across Asia in 1990 and held the Adidas rights until 1998. Thereafter, they launched the Umbro brand in Japan in 1999, although Umbro-branded kits had earlier been used by J.League teams. Regional shirt versions also come with their own sizing range. The Japanese Association of Sporting Goods Industries formulated a sizing guide which runs S, M, L as per European guides but then adds O (*ōkī* – large), XO (extra-large), 2XO, etc. The sizes run approximately two sizes smaller than their European equivalent. South American shirts run as T1, T2, T3, T4 ('T' representing *talla*, or size), with T1 equivalent to a UK small adult.

Japanese football expert Alan Gibson is from the West Midlands, but has lived in Japan for over 30 years. He runs *JSoccer Magazine*, an English language publication on Japanese football, while also helping overseas fans to obtain Japanese club and national team shirts. He explained that the domestic shirt retail market is very different to the stack-'em-high philosophy in the western European markets, 'In Japan in a sports store there will be plenty of European team shirts but it's often much harder to find a J1 [Japanese top-flight] team's jersey. If you want to guarantee a shirt you often need to make a pre-order. Shonan Bellmare [Hidetoshi Nakata's first side] are a good example; their shirts are rarely seen in shops, with the club selling them via very limited pre-orders only, direct from their website. There's usually a two-week window well before the season starts where you can order, and then the shirts are delivered just days before the new campaign kicks off. For the bigger teams they are more readily available, but supply is limited.' This is surprising given what Alan reveals about J.League fans' enthusiasm for their team's colours, 'At Japanese football games, if you don't have a shirt and scarf, you're not a proper fan!'

He explains the limited releases as a consequence of the low-risk corporate culture, 'The teams seem to aim for maximum profit at minimal risk, there are no discounts and very rarely any sales at the end of the season because they have all gone.' He even mentions severe consequences for a retailer who failed to adhere to this approach. 'Many years ago I had a friend who owned a football shirt shop and most of his shirts were from overseas suppliers, mostly in the UK. He'd buy them in bulk and get discount prices,' Alan reveals. 'He once managed to get hold of some J.League shirts and offered them at a small discount, and soon found that no one would sell them to him anymore and his supply soon dried up.'

In contrast to European teams offering replicas right throughout the professional pyramid and beyond, some third-tier J3 teams do not even take the 'risk' of offering small-volume replica versions of their shirts. At around ¥11,000 and up, equivalent to around £70, the shirt prices are similar but namesets are around ¥5,000, adding more than £30 to the purchase price. The namesets are also rarely sold in anything other than pre-made sets with established player names and numbers, so it is much more difficult for fans to add their own name or that of a retired player for example.

The environmental and social impact of replica shirt production is often lost amid the wall-to-wall daily reporting on football, despite the best efforts of campaign groups. The industry forms part of the larger footwear and clothing sector, which accounts for eight per cent of all environmental emissions according to a 2016 Quantis report, *Measuring Fashion*. Polyester is made from oil, and the process of developing the material and final garment results in around 5.5kg of carbon dioxide being produced for each shirt made. This compares to an estimated 2.3kg for a cotton T-shirt. Over 500,000 polyester fibres are released with each wash, finding their way to oceans and causing damage to ecosystems. At the end of each season, millions of pieces of unsold stock go to landfill. Given that polyester takes hundreds of years to decompose, this practice alone represents a substantial and persisting insult to the environment.

The growing focus on businesses' environmental impacts means that sustainability has become another key issue for manufacturers. Many now offer garments made from recycled materials to reduce the environmental impact of production. From 2010, Nike's polyester shirts have been made using up to eight recycled plastic bottles such that nearly ten billion bottles have been recovered from landfill. The firm's PR team supplied a creatively designed media kit to promote the innovation's launch, with a recycled club or national shirt presented within a plastic bottle. Nottingham firm PlayerLayer supply teams including Forest Green Rovers, who were recognised by FIFA and the United Nations as the world's 'greenest' team in 2017. The club are fully vegan including meals taken to away matches in their electric-powered coach, while the floodlights which shine on their organic pitch are powered in part by solar panels on one of the ground's stands. PlayerLayer offer eco-friendly shirts made from recycled coffee grounds or bamboo charcoal combined with recycled polyester.

Puma took the concept of recycled plastics a stage further in 2022, announcing their RE:JERSEY technology which allows the recycling of old shirts with embroidery and badges into new kits. However, few leading clubs have taken the obvious sustainability step announced by Brentford in their first Premier League season in 2021/22, by announcing a decision to retain their home shirt for the following campaign.

Another important consideration is the working conditions of those manufacturing shirts, which has been under scrutiny for over a quarter of a century. From the 1980s, sports manufacturers began to move production to the Far East, to take advantage of lower labour and production costs. Dave Moor views the offshoring of manufacturing as one of the most important changes in the history of football kit in the last 50 years. He recounts a story that would be familiar to domestic companies operating at the time, 'I remember having a conversation with the CEO of a company that operated in the south of England and manufactured a leading British team's shirts. At the end of the season, he had a call from the club's chairman to congratulate him because the club had made a million pounds. They then asked him whether he would be willing to drop his prices by 40 per cent otherwise they would move all their manufacturing to Vietnam! His reply was very brief.'

In the mid-1990s, mainstream media reports emerged of the use of child labour and poor working conditions for adults within sporting-goods factories in Pakistan and India. In 2000, this had escalated to a hearing organised by the European Parliament's Development Committee. They heard evidence that Adidas employed workers including children for long hours with poor pay in their Indonesian factories. The company was criticised for boycotting the hearing, sending a third-party representative without knowledge of the country's labour market.

Nike's own corporate responsibility report for 2007 to 2009 highlighted the scale of the problem, with over a third of their suppliers' factories surveyed being deemed noncompliant with serious system failures. Of these, 28 per cent were graded 'C' by Nike's own monitoring assessment, meaning issues such as failing to provide contracts, failure to meet local minimum wage or migrant labour laws, use of child labour, verbal or mental abuse of staff or requiring them to work long hours or seven days per week. Worse than this, six per cent were graded 'D' meaning offences such as use of indentured or prison labour, use of force to compel illegal work hours, widespread use of child labour, mandatory pregnancy testing or failure to provide legally required maternity leave. Furthermore, meaning management refusing to comply with standards, denying access to inspectors or providing false information to the company.

While most companies now have worker welfare strategies in place, data collected in 2020 by the EU-funded Clean Clothes Campaign suggest that standards are still not at an acceptable level with zero per cent of Puma, Adidas or Nike's factory workers paid a local living wage. As recently as 2022, an investigation by *The Mirror* newspaper revealed that workers producing England's £115 'authentic' Nike shirt earned the minimum wage of less than £1 per hour as part of a 60-hour week with no union to protect them.

The Collector

'YOU JUST catch the bug, don't you? Once you start a collection, you build that wish list and then you're hitting the same websites five or six times a day. It's just a passion that lives with you,' says Doug Bierton, co-founder of retailer Classic Football Shirts (CFS) and a self-confessed shirt-collecting addict.

The birth of the replica industry in the 1970s gave fans like Doug an opportunity to collect these footballing mementoes. This pastime was transformed at the end of the 20th century when the internet gave collectors greater access to far-flung clubs and national sides, allowing them to pick up notable designs from all corners of the world. In addition, the new technology allowed fans to share their passion and trade their shirts through forums, websites, and eventually social media.

The hobby remained a niche pursuit until the latter part of the 2010s, with all but the rarest vintage shirts available for less than the price of the current season's strip. However, the growth of vintage shirt retailers and the explosion in interest in the topic across social media saw prices increase dramatically. Doug and CFS co-founder Matt Dale discussed their experiences observing the development of the shirt-collecting scene close up since starting their business in 2006. Matt said, 'I think it's just much more culturally acceptable to wear a football shirt today. Even five to six years ago, you wouldn't necessarily want to walk down the street in a current shirt. Now you see the manufacturers promoting them much more, and they're popping up in music videos.' Doug added, 'Football shirts have become so mainstream, from being an underground thing to everyone wanting to talk about their collection online which is amazing! But you would have never predicted that ten years ago.'

This interest peaked during the Covid-19 pandemic as football fans stuck at home redirected money that would usually be spent on attending matches and other social activities into buying vintage polyester. The first shirt that CFS sold on their website in 2006 was a Liverpool 1988/89 shirt, which cost £64.99. As an illustration of how prices have boomed in the past few years, a search of leading retailers in February 2023 showed prices from £350 to £450 for the same shirt. In addition to replica shirts, a hardy group of experts seek out match-worn versions, with their prices often many times higher than the commercial releases.

Throughout the 1990s, most early collectors bought and sold shirts at car boot sales, vintage and charity shops and memorabilia fairs. The internet boom and birth of eBay gave collectors worldwide an opportunity to securely trade shirts internationally for the first time. Many prominent figures in the shirt-collecting world were involved with this platform in its infancy. Kit expert, collector and seller Peris Hatton explained that there were only around 250 shirts up for sale at a time on

UK eBay in the early 2000s, whereas a search for Lancashire club Burnley's jerseys alone now returns over 1,000 listings, 'There were a couple of other people like myself selling 15 to 20 shirts at a time, but otherwise it was people listing single shirts as part of a clear-out. How eBay's grown and helped to evolve the hobby is incredible, because there was no real way to sell shirts to collectors before that time. It's made it possible for hundreds of thousands of people like us to get our hands on the millions of shirts that are still out there. There are now other retailers and platforms, but if you want something old or obscure it's still the best place.' Doug Bierton also recounted his earliest experiences on the auction site, which he and Matt used to trade shirts prior to establishing their first website in 2006, 'Back then it was difficult to get pictures, you'd maybe get a poor-quality digital camera shot if you were lucky.'

The advent of dedicated retailers was another important development for shirt collecting, as collectors could buy shirts without having to develop an in-depth knowledge of how to discern genuine from counterfeit items on auction sites. CFS are giants of the replica shirt industry, with a turnover of more than £18m in 2021 and their Manchester and London stores complemented by a 70,000-square-foot warehouse in east Manchester. The company have since been joined by the likes of Vintage Football Shirts (founded 2010), Cult Kits and NI CLASICO in the UK, Le Sette Sorelle ('The Seven Sisters' in Italian, referring to a group of the largest clubs in the 1990s) in Italy, and RB Jerseys in Belgium. CFS's warehouse is football shirt geek heaven, with row after row of shirts from clubs and national teams around the globe. Such is the scale of the operation that staff involved in picking orders use electric scooters to travel around. In addition to the replica and kit-room stock, the building houses an incredible collection of thousands of match-worn shirts in a climate-controlled room. This includes the oldest jersey in the company's possession, a 1951 England away shirt worn by Sir Tom Finney against Argentina, which was the first red shirt worn by the team.

Matt and Doug founded CFS in 2006 while at university, after Doug sold an England 1990 shirt for £50 that he had bought for £5 for a fancy-dress night. While the business started slowly, trading a Mark Hughes Manchester United match-worn shirt for a collection of 20 years of the team's replicas helped to propel its growth. Another key moment was when an Italian contact located 250,000 items of unworn kit in AC Milan's warehouse which CFS bought in 2010. While the company now has a recognisable corporate structure, in the early days it was much more freewheeling; Matt recalled lending a match-worn Johan Cruyff Washington Dips shirt to pals to wear on a night out.

CFS have begun to reach out into the mainstream, partnering with broadcaster BT Sport to produce the *What I Wore* TV series since 2018 where current and ex-footballers including Paul Gascoigne, Pep Guardiola, Patrick Vieira and Harry Kane discuss strips from important parts of their career taken from the company's warehouse. More recently, the firm's Born in the 90s collection of shirts designed by Cassidy Sepnieski featured in the *FIFA 22* video game and from the 2022/23 they became the main shirt sponsor for Burnley.

Previous Borussia Dortmund shirts had featured rich woven jacquard patterns, such as the adapted Nike Premier logo (top) in the 1994/95 home shirt and a list of the club's major trophies in the 2009 centenary shirt (bottom). Credit: Richard Kelly

Neymar is the latest star name to wear Brazil's number 10 jersey, with previous holders including Pelé, Zico, Rivaldo, Ronaldinho and Kaká.

Player namesets were widely adopted in the 1990s, and the fonts themselves have become markers of a particular era. This Umbro style was also used by the England national team during their unsuccessful bid for European Championship glory on home soil in 1996. Credit: Richard Kelly

The reigning Italian Serie A champions have worn a scudetto ('little shield') patch since 1924 (bottom left), with the Italian Cup holders sporting a round 'coccarda' since 1958. In the 1990s, the development of competition branding saw sleeve patches become popular. Credit: Richard Kelly

Football shirts have attracted a host of famous fans, including Queen's Freddie Mercury in this Le Coq Sportif Argentina home jersey in 1981.

Special-edition shirts featuring club-specific detailing also began to appear in the last decade. Credit: Richard Kelly

Admiral's groundbreaking deal with Leed United saw copyrighted, branded kits appear on the pitch in the 1973/74 season, with the first real replica versions being sold to young fans.

The world's most famous shirt swap – Sir Bobby Moore and Pelé, following Brazil's 1-0 group-stage victory over England at the 1970 World Cup.

Diego Maradona's shirt, worn in the 'Hand of God' match against England in 1986, was sold for £7.1m at auction in 2022.

Football shirt heaven – one section of retailer Classic Football Shirts' 70,000 sq. ft. warehouse.

A future classic. A replica version of Argentina's World Cup 2022-winning shirt, with Lionel Messi's nameset and a competition patch. The federation crest features two stars commemorating the nation's World Cup victories in 1978 and 1986, with another star to be added following the team's recent triumph. Credit: Richard Kelly

Football shirts and shirt collecting have moved into the mainstream since the start of the 2010s, being evident in areas such as festival culture as well as on the high street. The move has also been supported by high-profile celebrities donning football strips. The latter is not only a modern development, with Bob Marley snapped playing five-a-side against then Ligue 1 champions Nantes while wearing the team's strip back in 1980. Music stars like Marley have adopted the football shirt both on and off stage. US political revolutionaries Rage Against the Machine appeared on a Belgian concert stage in 1994 in the nation's World Cup strip, while iconic images of Michael Jackson in an OGC Nice jersey and Queen's lead singer Freddie Mercury partying with Diego Maradona while wearing an Argentina shirt have also surfaced. Undoubtedly the king of the celebrity shirt fan is rapper Snoop Dogg, who often picks up football shirts as a memento of cities visited on tour, even wearing them on stage. His collection features a diverse range of sides from Manchester United, Real Madrid and Ajax to Burnley, Croatia and Cardiff City.

These celebrity endorsements can have a huge impact on a shirt's popularity, such as when singer Drake posted a photo of himself in a pink Juventus 2015/16 away jersey. As Matt Dale explained, 'We had a few thousand of them in clearance. For whatever reason they weren't that popular, but then a couple of years later they took on a life of their own partly because Drake wore one. We were selling them for £29.99, and now if you find a brand-new one with tags it's five to seven times that only a few years on.' As a more recent example, Kim Kardashian was photographed in a Roma 1997/98 home shirt in January 2023. Over the following week, Google searches for Roma increased nearly thirty-fold and multiple eBay listings of the shirt appeared at inflated prices with the name 'Kardashian' in the keywords.

Having made the decision to start a kit collection, the collector is faced with an almost limitless number of shirts available. For over 30 years, thousands of clubs and over 100 national sides have been releasing home, away, third and even 13th kits in the case of Napoli in 2021/22. To focus their search, many kit collectors choose to assemble their collection around a particular theme. This could be collecting their favourite team's jerseys, perhaps from the collector's year of birth onwards or from the season they first began to watch the team. David Beckham superfan Scott Anderson has collected all the club shirts worn by his favourite player, from his loan to Third Division Preston North End in 1994/95 to his final season with Paris Saint-Germain in 2012/13. Some collectors focus on a particular competition, as Rob Fletcher did in 2020. He successfully collected all the shirts worn by the victor in the Champions League Final going back to the competition's rebranding in 1992, with Milan's white 1994 shirt completing the collection. Others take a more *laissez-faire* attitude in their collection, such as Dutch collector Arjan Wijngaard. Having first been gifted an Everton shirt in 1997, he has since built up a collection of over 3,000 club and national shirts from around the world.

One of the most challenging collections to complete is acquiring a shirt from each of the more than 200 national sides that are FIFA members. Joe Johnston is one of the few to have achieved this. He began during the 2010 World Cup after seeing his friend pick up exotic strips cheaply from charity shops. Joe went into an Oxfam store and emerged with the Scotland and Slovenia jerseys. With an Argentina shirt at home already, he realised that his three pieces formed the start of a possible collection, with internet research showing that the number of FIFA nations then stood at 208. He started a blog, The Global Obsession, on which he charted his progress, and through social media he found a small group of like-minded individuals attempting the same feat. This already tricky task was made more challenging by the fact that the member list is constantly evolving, such as South Sudan being added in 2012.

While eBay was initially a good source of the more readily available strips, in many cases shirts were not available commercially. Joe contacted footballers, embassies, national associations, and sports shops from different countries to locate match-worn or low-volume replica versions with various acts of generosity and serendipity helping him towards his goal. Joe was sent a match-worn Mauritania shirt by a filmmaker from the country, while Monserrat international and Lowestoft Town player Dean Mason brought him back his match-worn shirt from a World Cup qualifier. Most incredible was the former owner of an Azerbaijan under-17 squad-signed shirt that Joe unearthed on eBay. He found out that the date and place name written on the jersey was from a tournament at which the team had an audience with Pope Benedict XVI and presented the original owner with the shirt. How it found its way from His Holiness to an online auction site is unknown.

Joe and his fellow FIFA challengers developed a camaraderie and offered support to each other, such as when in a leap of faith Joe wired a large sum of money to a Malawian sports shop and was rewarded with a delivery of 15 Malawi shirts which he distributed to his fellow collectors. After seven years, Joe took delivery of a Madagascar shirt in June 2017 to complete his collection. Both the hunt itself and its completion had attracted international media attention with outlets from Albania to Algeria covering the story alongside dozens of UK newspapers, radio and TV stations. The efforts of Joe and his fellow collectors have been sufficient to motivate several nations, who did not previously make their shirts commercially available, to manufacture small-volume replica shirt runs in response to an increasing number of enquiries from would-be members of the FIFA shirt club.

As writer and kit collector John Blair detailed in a series of articles for *KIT Magazine*, there are several factors which determine a second-hand shirt's price. Most obviously, the age of the shirt is a key factor as greater availability of modern shirts means that there is a larger supply. In addition, many shirts are worn to destruction by their owners so the pool of available shirts from each year decreases with time. Typically, common shirts from the 1990s will be two to three times the price of a modern shirt. Intertwined with this is the shirt's condition, as wear in the form of bobbles, plucks and holes are common and name and numbersets can wear easily. Some shirts have specific features prone to damage, such that finding a rare example intact often comes at a premium. Manchester United's 2007 to 2009 home shirt (worn as they won the Champions League in 2008) had two white plastic stripes at the top and bottom of the reverse side. These features, also included on the away shirt, commonly detached even after careful washing and only a minority of shirts retained the feature intact, thereby attracting a premium price.

Some collectors retain their shirts in brand-new condition with the original sales tags attached which can increase the price by more than 20 per cent relative even to a 'de-tagged' shirt in excellent condition. Incredibly some shirts released 30 years or more ago are still unearthed in 'brand new with tags' (BNWT) condition. Even these marketing devices themselves can be very nostalgic. An example is a Juventus 1994/95 home shirt picked up in this condition with half a dozen tags clustered around the collar. Anyone who was at school during the 1990s will remember the blue rectangular 'PEOPLE ON THE MOVE' (*GENTE IN MOVIMENTO* in the Italian version) collar tag sticker which littered almost every desk, bag and other available surface mid-decade.

Peris Hatton seems to have an inexhaustible supply of these vintage shirts in brand-new condition which he showcases on his popular Twitter account. He finds the rare sight of a fully boxed kit set very emotive, 'I've been lucky enough to handle a few of these over the years, and I've still got a couple in the collection. When I post one of them on social media, the response I get is phenomenal. A whole kit in a box … imagine how excited you would have been getting that as an eight- or nine-year-old on Christmas morning. And then the box gets ripped to pieces because you can't wait to get to what's inside, and so few survive today.'

The popularity of the team is also a factor, with shirts from the likes of Manchester United, Barcelona and Juventus attracting a premium over those of teams with a lower profile. Rarer shirts understandably have a higher price, such as those which were not released commercially or only in a limited number. For example, Borussia Dortmund did not offer any of their four Nike away shirts from 1990 to 1994 for sale to fans. As a result, on the rare occasion that a shirt originally from kit-room stock appears on auction sites ,they cost upwards of £400 to £500 whereas the corresponding home shirts and later away shirts can typically be found for £60 to £120. The club also released only 9,009 'blackout' shirts to commemorate their 110th anniversary in 2019, and rare examples of the boxed shirt change hands for £400 to £500 or more only four years after its release. The shirt design itself can be a key determinant, as demand for those seen as iconic drives the price up. Arsenal's 'Bruised Banana' typically sells for £200 to £300, around three times that of the club's other shirts from the same era. Even an iconic sponsor alone can cause a strip's price to rocket, Fiorentina's 1997 to 1999 deal with video-game manufacturer Nintendo making shirts from that era at least twice as expensive as those sporting Toyota's or ice-cream maker Sammontana's logo from the same period.

The advent of namesets in the mid-1990s led to another source of shirt rarity, as only a subset of shirts sold had printing and even then the choice of player provided additional variability. Of particular interest and value are clubs' and national teams' most beloved players, with a Barcelona Messi, Fiorentina Batistuta, or Inter Milan Ronaldo shirt among the most sought-after. Shirts worn by players at their first club or when first assigned a higher squad number as a youth player are also highly prized, Messi's number 30 shirt from the 2005/06 season and Kylian Mbappé's number 29 from his breakthrough 2016/17 season at Monaco both attracting higher bids than shirts from later in their career.

A shirt's size affects its value, with the most popular medium and large sizes attracting a premium, although would-be collectors need to consider the sizing in different eras when purchasing vintage shirts. Particularly in the 1990s the fit was much more generous than today, so depending on the desired look collectors may be able to wear a shirt two or three sizes smaller than their modern equivalent. For more compact collectors, they may be able to squeeze into youth-sized shirts which commonly measure like a modern adult small size. It must be noted that the youth shirts may differ slightly in their design with smaller crests, manufacturer's logo or sponsors common but they usually command a price 25 to 50 per cent lower than adult versions as a result.

Many collectors now look at their shirts as an investment, having seen the rapid growth in prices over the past few years. Matt Dale had a surprising recommendation for those looking to invest in modern shirts. 'Maybe some of the designs that are being criticised now, like the Puma third shirts,' he suggested.

'If you're going to invest in a shirt, I would get a Haaland shirt with the BVB [2021/22] European design. When you think, "What reminds me of Haaland at that time?", it's that shirt. If you're going to get a shirt, get it with a nameset because those are the ones in time that will be worth more.' While Puma's designs were not well received by fans, Matt makes a comparison with another shirt now viewed as a classic, 'There was a really bad reaction to the "Bruised Banana" at the time. There will be people who look at the whole [Puma 2021/22 third] collection and want to find a Shakhtar one or a Valencia one.' While it is early in their history, and indeed some of the strips are still available commercially, certainly the number of social media posts from collectors looking for less common shirts from the collection such as the Independiente and Shakhtar versions is increasing.

Would-be collectors must also pick through the fakes which have flooded the market in recent years. As discussed in 'The Replica', counterfeit shirts have been available almost as long as the real thing, with many collectors holding memories of cheap strips picked up in popular holiday destinations. These shirts, mass-produced in the 1980s and 1990s, made little claim to be authentic items. Like a police-sketch version of the genuine article, they contained most of the relevant features such as the sponsor and crest but of such low quality that even the greenest buyer could not mistake them for the real deal. As the replica market continued to grow at the turn of the millennium, the quality of reproductions improved. Today, on first inspection many fake strips are indistinguishable from the real thing. It is only when expert eyes take a closer look that issues like stitching quality and subtle differences in the design of the crest and manufacturer mark a garment out as inauthentic. The growing value of vintage shirts has made reproductions of these items another profitable avenue for rogue manufacturers. On an eBay trawl for a Fiorentina Nintendo shirt or the Manchester United 1992–1994 third 'Newton Heath' strip, the number of fraudulent items far outweighs the number of real listings that appear.

A further challenge to original collectors has been the proliferation of providers of imitation period namesets. For those collectors wanting to add another layer of personalisation to their collection, they can now find namesets in the style of the time so that Ronaldo, Cantona or Batistuta adorn their vintage strip. Finally, the availability of basic template shirts identical to those used by famous teams means that with just a couple of printed details a nondescript £50 Adidas Ipswich template becomes a Netherlands 1988 shirt with a sale value of ten to 20 times that price. Multiple prominent examples of this DIY craftsmanship have been floating around the online kit fan community for the past few years. First, several blue Netherlands Ipswich templates have been claimed as a rare away version and commanded high prices when there is no record of such a design being made officially. Similarly, the popularity of the short-lived Nintendo Fiorentina sponsorship fuelled high prices for a series of training shirts featuring the brand's icon Mario, although they were later found out to be inauthentic.

While these issues present challenges to even the most seasoned collectors, there are several steps that would-be buyers can take to avoid forking out for an expensive fake. Buying from established retailers will minimise the risk of being duped, although many have unwittingly been found to have offered counterfeit items for sale. Some obvious clues are found in the listings themselves. While occasionally a mint condition, decades-old shirt surfaces complete with tags, a listing with multiple versions of the same shirt in different sizes should certainly arouse suspicion. Incongruence between the condition of different elements of the garment is also a helpful guide; if a shirt appears with plenty of pulls and bobbles but a pristine nameset, then the latter is likely a recent addition.

There are also a few clues that collectors look for within certain brands – the texture of a 1990s Umbro tag and the collection of dots on a Kappa label from the same period are features not duplicated by replica manufacturers. For more recent shirts, the product codes contained in the neck label of Adidas shirts and washing labels of other brands give strong evidence of a top's authenticity. Googling the middle number on these tags should bring back multiple pictures of the item it claims to be. If other club or country strips are more common in the search findings, it is almost certain to be counterfeit. If genuine, the cardboard swing tag should also include the genuine code and details of the team and home/away/third shirt. So ubiquitous are these fakes that common counterfeit codes have become well known by collectors, the code P95985 accompanied by the generic swing tag description ADIDAS JSY being the most common. One final quick clue is that for reasons of cost and effort, where the original had a woven jacquard fabric, phoney jerseys will usually sublimate or print the pattern instead.

Unfortunately, beyond these simple tips, the only reliable way to compare a shirt to the real deal is to have one in hand or at least detailed pictures of a genuine article for comparison. While this might be challenging for a new collector, invariably more established shirt fans (having all experienced the frustration of buying a fake at some point) are only too happy to help provide these details to spare others the same fate. A final point of consolation is that online markets such as eBay usually offer a high level of protection for customers. If a shirt turns out to be fake, they will allow buyers to return with the seller footing the cost of return postage.

The rarity of match-worn shirts means that those worn in football's most famous moments command massive fees way beyond those paid for replicas, on the rare occasions that they are traded publicly. Diego Maradona's shirt from the 1986 World Cup quarter-final against England attracted global media attention when it was put up for auction in May 2022. The Argentinian maestro had scored two memorable goals in the game: first, his 'Hand of God' when he used his hand to put the ball past England goalkeeper Peter Shilton; four minutes later he dribbled past half of the England team having started the move in his own half to score one of the finest goals in football history. These dual claims to fame likely explain the massive £7.1m winning auction bid when England player Steve Hodge, with whom Maradona had swapped shirts after the game, put the item up for sale.

Maradona's shirt managed to command a high fee despite not being an official Argentina strip. While the team had been supplied with an Aertex fabric home shirt to help them cope with the heat in host country Mexico, the change strip was a standard cotton shirt which also became very heavy in the wet conditions in which the team faced off against Uruguay in the round of 16. With the prospect of facing England in the unsuitable garment, the team requested a more lightweight jersey but were told that this could not be supplied in time. Incredibly, team coach Carlos Bilardo set about the change tops with a pair of scissors, aiming to replicate the perforated Aertex fabric. This was not the only time that Argentina's staff would modify their shirt, later being forced to adapt defender José Luis Brown's shirt in the final against West Germany. Having scored the opening goal, Brown dislocated his shoulder towards the end of the match but refused to leave the field. A hole was cut in the middle of his shirt, allowing him to hook his thumb inside, fashioning a makeshift sling.

Returning to the quarter-final, it became apparent that Bilardo's homemade ventilation was not a viable solution and the team's technical assistant Rubén Moschella was dispatched into Mexico City to find some more lightweight alternatives. Having scoured around 40 stores, he returned with two strips, Maradona choosing the lighter of the two with the words, 'That one. We'll beat England in that one.'

Moschella returned to purchase 38 shirts, but the outdated templates contained no crest or even squad numbers. A designer created some makeshift federation badges, which were hastily sewed on. The only numbers which the team could track down were glittery silver and designed for American football. In his autobiography *Touched by God*, Maradona described the chaotic scenes prior to their famous victory, 'And the numbers, the numbers were a joke. When we went out on to the field, some of the guys had sparkles on their face. And after genius kit man Tito Benrós had ironed those numbers on to 38 jerseys, he looked like he should have been at carnival, not at Azteca stadium! If it happened to rain, like it had in our match against Uruguay, it was going to be a real disaster: we wouldn't know who was who or what position the others were playing. So with our hand and faces covered in sparkles, we went to sleep at 11 o'clock that night. And the game was early the next morning.' An inauspicious start for what would become the world's most expensive sporting relic 36 years later.

The fee dwarfed the previous record of £157,750 set in 2002 for Pelé's shirt worn in Brazil's 1970 World Cup Final victory. The record had been set to be broken by Sir Geoff Hurst's shirt worn as he scored a hat-trick to win England their only World Cup, in 1966. However, the shirt failed to make its £300,000 reserve price at auction in 2016, having previously changed hands for £91,750 in 2008. Given their prominent places in the history of football, it is perhaps not surprising that England and Brazil shirts feature so prominently in the list of high-value auction items. A classic photo of Pelé and Bobby Moore embracing after Brazil's 1-0 group-stage victory over England en route to their victory in 1970 also shows the pair holding their exchanged match shirts. Moore's jersey fetched £59,750 in 2004 while the Brazilian's top (by now in very poor condition) only commanded a price of £4,320 in 2007.

Looking much further back in football history, striker Rupert Darnley Anderson played one match for England as a goalkeeper in 1879. His strip, worn in England's first match against Wales which also saw the Welsh side's first goal, sold for £17,750 in 2022. While international shirts dominate the highest-value slots, some club strips also have the potential to command large fees. The shirt worn by Manchester City striker Sergio Agüero in which he scored an injury-time goal to win the Premier League title in 2012 was put up for auction in 2022. Having attracted pre-auction bids of nearly £50,000, it was withdrawn from sale amid doubts about its provenance. Even shirts which saw no on-pitch action can have substantial value, like the replica strip sported by Mesut Özil during his signing ceremony for Fenerbahçe – which reached £23,000 at auction in 2021.

While shirts like Maradona's 1986 strip have a direct line of providence from the dressing room to the auction house, for others the path is more complicated. Collectors are often dependent on unofficial certificates of authenticity (COAs) written by companies, or personal letters from the original or even subsequent recipients attesting to the garment's origins. Amateur detective work can be employed to compare distinctive features such as damage, wear or even mud patterns to match footage and photography. Into this unregulated space arrived AC Momento in 2022, the US firm attracting $20m in funding for its match-worn shirt auction and content platform. Partnering with clubs including AC Milan, Sevilla, Atlético Madrid and Benfica, the firm gave fans a chance to buy match-worn shirts during the live games in which they were being worn through their app. Once the match had concluded, Momento's staff would pick up the shirt direct from the dressing room and transfer it to a secure vault in London or Madrid. It then underwent a 'curation' process, as moisture and bacteria were removed, and the shirt was deodorised. An authentication label, including a QR code which links to a digital COA, was affixed to the shirt and professional photos of the front and back were taken and added to the digital COA. The buyer then had the option to 'redeem' the shirt and have it sent to them in Momento packaging. Alternatively, they could store the shirt in climate-controlled vaults more commonly used to store priceless artworks and jewellery.

Momento also partnered with players to store and display their personal collections accumulated throughout their career. For new match-worn shirts, Momento had a direct evidence trail back to the locker room and could certify them with 100 per cent authority. However, for items in a player's collections, Momento's experts sat with a player and gathered the evidence needed to assess a shirt's authenticity. These investigations revealed significant features about the shirt that weren't evident at the time. For example, Dani Alves owned a Ronaldinho Barcelona shirt that he swapped with him post-match as a young player at Sevilla. When authenticating the shirt, Momento realised that this was Ronaldinho's debut appearance for Barça.

Although well funded and resourced, the first year of Momento's operation showed the challenges which have prevented the broader development of the match-worn market. The time and cost requirements of the authentication process needed to ensure shirts' provenance proved prohibitive. In addition, for auctions of Argentina and Spain shirts during the 2022 World Cup, the company faced challenges in securing and authenticating match-worn tops. As a result, in March 2023 they withdrew from auctioning and storing such items. It must be recognised that some clubs have also worked independently to improve the security of match-worn purchases. In 2019, Fiorentina collaborated with Genuino to use blockchain technology to authenticate match-worn shirts from games against Inter on 15 December and Roma on 20 December via a tag fixed to the shirt. Other clubs provide a unique code which can be used by a purchaser to link the shirt to a database of official match-worn items sold directly to fans.

To replica shirt collectors, the match-worn shirt scene is a mysterious entity completely removed from hunting through eBay and picking up end-of-season bargains. West Ham fan and match-worn shirt-collector Mick Clifford gave some insights on what is required to hunt down these precious relics. Mick is English but has lived in Sweden for many years and has assembled an incredible collection of over 600 match-worn shirts. 'I don't have a 1975 FA Cup Final shirt, otherwise I have one from each of West Ham's modern FA Cup finals, Charity Shield matches, the two Cup Winners' Cup and three Championship play-off finals,' Mick explained. A few years ago, West Ham ran a fan poll to find the best 16 players to play for the club. Of these, Mick had 15 players' shirts with only Martin Peters – who played for the Hammers from 1961 to 1970 – evading him. Mick said, 'If one came up I don't think I'd be able to afford it!'

Some of the incredible tales Mick told paint a vivid picture of the creative thinking and persistence that is required to track them down. 'When I started it was in the early 1990s so there was no internet, it involved ringing clubs and trying to get old players' phone numbers or information,' he explained. 'I have a 1980 FA Cup Final shirt from West Ham's number nine David Cross, who I knew had swapped with Arsenal's number six Willy Young. I called Young's next club Nottingham Forest and asked them if they knew anything about where he was after he'd stopped playing. They told me he owned a pub and hotel in the Nottingham area and gave me the phone number. I couldn't just call him and ask him for his shirt, so I flew over and booked two nights in his hotel hoping he'd be there. He was, and I talked to him about his career, his shirts and we got on to the cup final shirt and I asked him if I could purchase it from him. It took a couple of days persuading him to sell it to me; in the end he gave it to me as a reward for my persistence after I told him I'd flown over from Sweden, and I was only in the hotel to get the shirt. He thought I was crazy! At the time they weren't very expensive when they came up at auction. I don't think he'd have given it to me nowadays as that shirt would be worth ten to £15,000!'

That shirts had little sale value explains some of the older players attitudes to them, as exemplified by another incredible experience Mick had with former Belgian international François Van der Elst. After being interviewed, François made a joke about giving Mick his 1976 West Ham shirt from the Cup Winners' Cup Final (at that point missing from Mick's collection) if Mick would visit him at home in Brussels. Mick took him at his word, flew to Belgium and took a taxi to Van der Elst's snooker hall. Although taken aback by his surprise visitor, the former Anderlecht player invited him back to his home for dinner. Afterwards, he brought down three bin bags from his attic and tipped out his huge career match-worn collection. Among the gems were a Diego Maradona Argentina shirt, as well as those worn by Lothar Matthäus for West Germany and the Netherlands' Johnny Rep. Being typically bold, Mick asked to try them on and François agreed. 'Unfortunately I didn't have my camera with me,' said Mick, 'so I have the memories but not the evidence!' Having located the West Ham shirt, Mick's host then unceremoniously shoved what would now represent hundreds of thousands of pounds' worth of shirts back into the plastic sacks and stowed them back in his attic again.

In addition to persistence, luck and serendipity play a part. 'You have to know someone, ideally a player,' explained Mick. 'I know an ex-West Ham player and he's still in the team WhatsApp group. He's Swedish and I knew him from when he'd trained in the same lower-division side as my son. I thought, "Brilliant! I know this guy and he's gone to West Ham – unbelievable, what a piece of luck!" I have his Carabao Cup and Premier League debut shirts and the three shirts he wore when he was named as a substitute. If you don't have a contact at the club, it's very, very difficult.' The boom in football shirt collecting has also filtered through to the match-worn scene as Mick described, 'A few years back it was easier but now kids are holding up signs – "DECLAN RICE CAN I HAVE YOUR SHIRT?" The players will give the kids a shirt; it's a little more difficult when you're a 55-year-old man asking a 25-year-old player for his jersey! I have to explain to them about my collection and show them all the pictures on Instagram and in the end they come round. A few times I took my son, who asked Paolo Di Canio for me. He replied, "It's OK, I'll give it to your dad as I know it's him who wants it!"'

Many match-worn collectors see themselves as custodians of their clubs' history, taking on a task that these businesses are unwilling to do themselves. It has been a constant theme in my conversations with these collectors that they have approached their club for support and even offered their collection for loan and display but in the absence of a clear financial motive they are reluctant to engage. The same is true for replica kits, which could also be considered a valuable part of a club's heritage. 'There is no proper archive for all these old kits,' explained Peris Hatton. 'Umbro bought a few things off me around 2001 because they hadn't kept anything. It all needs to be on display somewhere. The National Football Museum do a brilliant job, but it could do with being about 50 times bigger to house all these wonderful shirts.' The latter point rings true regarding an experience unearthing a box at the museum's archives. Inside were around 50 brand-new shirts from the late 1990s, with beautiful jerseys from teams including Lazio, Anderlecht, Kaiser Chiefs, Guarani, Malmö,

Panathinaikos and Real Sociedad, all awaiting their turn on display in the Manchester city-centre showpiece.

It is not only fans who are keen to pick up their favourite players' strips, as shirt-swapping after matches has been common among players for decades. The first recorded occasion was in 1931, when at the seventh time of asking France beat England for the first time in a friendly match. The ecstatic victors asked the English players for their jerseys as a memento of the occasion, to which the disappointed opponents sportingly agreed. The practice did not become widespread in international football until the 1954 World Cup in Switzerland, perhaps due to the cost of replacement garments in what was still a relatively low-budget international game. This was particularly true in club football, an early example being Benfica icon Eusébio exchanging with his Real Madrid counterpart Alfredo Di Stéfano after the 1962 European Cup Final. Borne aloft by his exuberant team-mates after their victory, the Portuguese forward later revealed that he had stuffed the Argentinian's strip in his shorts and was terrified of the prospect of the precious garment falling out during the celebrations.

On occasion, pre-existing rivalries or particularly fiery games have prevented the post-game exchange, as when England manager Sir Alf Ramsey refused to allow his stars to swap with Argentina's players after a bruising quarter-final encounter in the 1966 World Cup. The practice is seen as a mark of respect between fellow professionals, exemplified by an iconic image of Pelé and Bobby Moore post-swap after a draw at the 1970 World Cup. The England captain joined a sizeable club of Pelé jersey owners, fed in part during the Brazilian's stint in the star-studded North American Soccer League during its 1970s heyday. Gordon Bradley, coach of New York Cosmos during Pelé's time at the club, recalled in an interview with the FIFA website, the huge demand for the Brazilian's shirt from opponents. 'Everyone wanted to change shirts with him,' he said, 'so we started taking about 25 to 30 shirts from him to distribute to the opposing team, otherwise we wouldn't be able to leave the stadium alive.' Earlier in his career, Pelé had attributed a loss of form to having given away his 'lucky' shirt to a fan of his club, Santos. The striker hired a detective who found the jersey and Pelé's on-field excellence returned, although it was later revealed that the detective never found the shirt and simply replaced it.

Given its eventual asking price at auction, Steve Hodge was lucky to procure Maradona's jersey thanks to a post-match interview. FIFA had banned shirt-swapping on the pitch for the 1986 World Cup to prevent players appearing topless in public. Hodge only bumped into Argentina's goalscorer following his media commitments. 'After the interview, I went down, behind the goal, to the changing rooms,' Hodge recalled on FIFA's website. 'As I went down, Maradona was walking with two of his team-mates. I looked him in the eye, tugged on my shirt as if to say, "Any chance of swapping?" and he came straight across, motioned a prayer, and we exchanged shirts. And that was it. It was just as simple as that.' Crucially, this meant that Hodge hadn't seen the 'Hand of God' incident at that point, and he explained, 'If I'd have known what had happened, I wouldn't have swapped my shirt with him.'

The Future

AFTER A fairly unremarkable evolution over the game's first century, the last 50 years has seen a revolution in the football shirt, rendering it unrecognisable from the simple cotton garment worn at the dawn of the 1970s. The birth of the replica industry and corporate sponsorships within that time has also led to the shirt becoming a key source of income particularly for leading clubs. Giants like Real Madrid now raise more from shirt sponsorship and replica kit deals than they do from supporters attending games. The pace of this change has been remarkable, and developments will continue. Below, several involved with football shirts have given their thoughts on how each aspect of the shirt will develop in the next decade. Having tracked the development of the football shirt over 150 years for this book, I also put forward a few speculative predictions.

Starting with **the shirt** itself, football finance expert Kieran Maguire predicted a desire to incorporate wearable technology into the garment to try to engage fans more with what is happening on the pitch. He cited the recent example of Manchester City's Connected Scarf developed in partnership with Cisco which tracked fan emotions through measuring blood pressure, heart rate and body temperature using an Emotibit biosensor. I agree with Kieran's prediction that wearable technologies will become integrated into both player and fan versions. On the player side, they could form another layer of the seemingly endless metrics pored over by armchair analysts. For fans, they offer a chance to measure their psychophysiological response to stressful in-game situations, in effect a digital picture of their mid-match emotions. Designer Craig Buglass is a huge advocate of kit sustainability and does not see current strategies as a long-term solution, 'While materials have evolved to become more sustainable, they are still made from recycled plastic bottles with holes in them. Billions of tonnes of polyester goes to landfill every year, it's scary and football needs to do its part. I would like companies to start looking at cellulosic fabrics and other solutions that have zero impact on our planet.'

Phil Delves suggested that the financial pressure of the big manufacturers could pressure UEFA and FIFA to relax their regulations and allow **the designs** to become much more innovative. This was a view shared by Denis Hurley, 'If we know anything at all about UEFA it's that money talks loudest, and with the constant threat of a breakaway [European] Super League they'll need to offer more flexibility. I can see the regulations being gradually eroded as with squad numbers. In 1996/97 squad numbers were introduced and players had to wear numbers 1-25 regardless of domestic regulations. Fast forward a few years and we have Vítor Baía winning the Champions League wearing number 99!'

Starting with the shirt itself, I think that we will continue to see further development of the huge impact that **the sponsor** has on shirt design. It seems inevitable at some point that the dam will break on international sponsors, perhaps driven by the women's game as part of efforts to attenuate inequalities in revenue. Also, new technology will lead to the erosion of fixed team sponsors as developments of Virtual Replacement Technology, which permits the pitchside adverts displayed to TV viewers to differ by territory, will allow similar opportunities for bespoke kit sponsorships.

Phil Delves suggested that we may see **the printing** become editable, as embedded electronics permit ongoing customisation of jerseys even after purchase. This could prevent cases whereby unexpected transfers, injury or even legal issues effectively make printed shirt worthless or certainly an unappealing prospect to wear. Related to this, I think that the growth of player 'brands', as evidenced by Cristiano Ronaldo's near-one billion followers across social media platforms, will lead to a greater degree of personal branding on shirts tied into the image-rights element of contracts.

Professor Jean Williams suggested that high-end fashion brands such as Burberry could be recruited by **the manufacturers** to design innovative kits, arriving as the likes of Nike originally did without preconceived ideas about what a football shirt looks like. She cited the example of Stella McCartney, who has designed an innovative collection for Arsenal's women's team including a pre-match shirt, following her work on the Team GB London 2012 Olympics teamwear for both sexes, including football shirts. This is supported by the entry of Emporio Armani as Napoli's kit supplier in 2021, and recent innovative collaborations such as that between the club and designer Marcelo Burton, between Juventus and skateboarding brand Palace, and Real Madrid and designer Yohji Yamamoto.

In terms of **the replica** market and kit collecting, it seems obvious that we will continue to see kits observe the 20 or 30-year rule, that high demand and associated prices of 1990s kits will fade and those of 2000s, 2010s, etc. will increase as those who came of age in those decades become financially independent. Kieran Maguire also predicted that clubs will get around the limitations of stadium capacity by using holographic technologies employed in recent music shows to 'resurrect' deceased artists. This would allow live broadcasts of matches in multiple ticketed venues simultaneously, with the opportunity to sell merchandising including shirts to a much larger 'match-going' crowd. To sate the need for at least three custom innovative kits each season, we will see more companies follow Puma's lead by subverting the established shirt design template.

Craig Buglass suggested that fan-led pressure relating to sustainability could see the return of strips lasting for more than one season, although the financial implications mean that prices will increase dramatically. In particular, those of the 'authentic' player-spec shirts, with the NFL – where changes are only permitted every five years and full-spec shirts can cost $350 – an extreme vision of the future. Given the growth in all sorts of collectable markets over the past few years and the popularity of football and shirt collecting, I am surprised that such little infrastructure for verification and trading of match-worn shirts exists. While AC Momento's Marketplace venture was not successful in its initial stage, I believe that more structured approaches like this will lead to greater confidence and interest in match-worns, with prices increasing as a result. Time will tell!

Acknowledgements

I AM extraordinarily grateful to a host of people who have supported me to bring this book together. My pal Rob Fletcher has been a constant source of support and encouragement, as we bludgeoned our way through our first attempts at writing a book. His excellent *1992: The Birth of Modern Football*, also published by Pitch, catalogues an extraordinary year encompassing the birth of the Premier League and Champions League, the introduction of the back-pass rule and a host of other developments which have shaped the modern game. I would also like to thank editors including Feargal McEvoy of *Halb Vier*, Stephen Fishlock of *World Soccer* and Andy Mitten of *United We Stand* for giving me the opportunity to contribute pieces to their publications. Without those experiences, I would probably still be yet to dip my toe into the world of football writing. In the same vein, thanks to Paul and Jane at Pitch Publishing for supporting this book project. Fellow kit writers Les Motherby and Phil Harrison have also been a source of encouragement, and no small amount of kit- and football history-related knowledge to boot! Les, Denis Hurley, Jonathan Rawcliffe and Rob also spent a lot of time to review the draft and made a series of very helpful corrections and suggestions for additional material which were very gratefully received. Richard Kelly was kind enough to offer his photographic skills to create many of the images in the plate section, supported by Sarah Collins's shirt-folding expertise! Thanks to Duncan Olner for his beautiful cover design, and to Gareth Davis for editing the book. Ian Leask, Chris Ireland and Angela Lynes were also invaluable sources of advice for a new author.

More broadly, the kind words, retweets and feedback on articles, podcasts and posts by members of the football kit community on Twitter have been an essential fuel throughout the process. This is not an exhaustive list, but fizzy lager enthusiast Kenny Legg, Stefan Appenowitz, the Shirt Union lads, CSGB, Cornish Kit Collector, Josh Butler, Zekey and Gav Hope have all done their bit. Several expert interviewees who gave up their time to discuss their pet topics added valuable contributions to the work. Peris Hatton, Phil Delves, Dave Moor, Kieran Maguire, Chris Oakley, Professor Jean Williams, Alan Gibson, John Devlin, Denis Hurley, Ben Houston, Doug Bierton, Matt Dale, Mick Clifford, Joe Johnston, Craig Buglass, Ffion Appleton-Jones and Stew Scott-Curran all contributed in this way, and I am very grateful for their input.

Many thanks also to Matt Leach for introducing me to the online kit sphere, and Jonathan Rawcliffe for sharing his professional journalism knowledge with an enthusiastic amateur. Importantly, to my dad for introducing me to Manchester United 30 years ago, a topic that continues to dominate almost every conversation we have had since! Likewise, my mum's patient tolerance as new shirts are paraded before her, and her enthusiasm and pride in the few minor achievements I have accomplished are both appreciated. Finally, while their input directly to the book has been limited, as always my wife Emma and sons Marco and Felix are a source of far greater joy than even football shirts can provide.

Bibliography

Books and journal articles:

Appenowitz, S., *Bundesliga Trikots 1963 bis heute* (Munich: GeraMond, 2018)

Benzecry, C., (2008) *Azul y Oro: The Many Social Lives of a Football Jersey*, Theory, Culture & Society, 25:1, 49–76, DOI: 10.1177/0263276407085158

Devlin, J., *True Colours: Football Kits from 1980 to the Present Day* (London: A&C Black, 2005)

Devlin, J., *International Football Kits (True Colours): The Illustrated Guide* (London: Bloomsbury, 2018)

Goldblatt, D., *The Ball is Round: A Global History of Football* (London: Penguin, 2006)

Heard, N., *The Football Shirts Book: The Connoisseur's Guide* (London: Ebury Press, 2017)

Hofmann, V., (2016) *Why We Wear It: the Football Shirt as a Badge of Identity*, New Ethnographies of Football in Europe, 176–191

Hurley, D., *Football Type 2* (Manchester: Face37, 2020)

Johnson, R., *The A-Z of Weird & Wonderful Football Shirts: Broccoli, Beers & Bruised Bananas* (Leicester: Conker Editions, 2020)

Kendall, G. & Osbaldiston, N. (2010) *'You're not fit to wear the shirt': towards a cultural sociology of the football shirt,* Social Causes, Private Lives: Proceedings of The Australian Sociological Association Conference, 1-12

Riley, M., *Kit & Caboodle* (Chichester: Pitch, 2022)

Routledge, M., & Wills, E., *The Beautiful Badge: The Stories Behind the Football Club Badge* (Chichester: Pitch, 2018)

Steinert, M., *Die Trikotgeschichte von Borussia Dortmund: Das BVB 09-Trikot in Wandel der Zeit* (Munich: GeraMond, 2019)

Stride, C., Williams, J., Moor, D. & Catley, N. (2015) *From Sportswear to Leisurewear: The Evolution of English Football League Shirt Design in the Replica Kit Era*, Sport in History, 35:1, 156-194, DOI: 10.1080/17460263.2014.986518

Stride, C., Catley, N. & Headland, J. (2020) *Shirt tales: how adults adopted the replica football kit, Sport in History*, 40:1, 106-146, DOI: 10.1080/17460263.2019.1578255

Wells, A., *Get Shirty: The Rise & Fall of Admiral Sportswear* (Leicester: Conker Editions, 2022)

Websites:

https://www.classicfootballshirts.co.uk
https://www.footballkitarchive.com
https://footballshirtcollective.com
https://www.footyheadlines.com
https://www.historicalkits.co.uk
https://kitbliss.co.nz
https://museumofjerseys.com
https://www.nssmag.com/en/sports/
https://www.oldfootballshirts.com/
https://www.passionemaglie.it
https://www.squadnumbers.com
https://www.truecoloursfootballkits.com